WISCONSIN TRAILS

GREAT WEEKEND ADVENTURES

FAVORITE GETAWAYS, FESTIVALS & EVENTS

FROM THE EDITORS OF
WISCONSIN TRAILS MAGAZINE

First edition, first printing
Copyright @ 1996 by Wisconsin Tales and Trails, Inc.

All rights reserved. No part of this publication may be reproduced or transmitted in any form or by any means, electronic or mechanical, including photocopying and recording, or by any information storage or retrieval system, without permission in writing from the publisher.

Library of Congress Catalog Card Number: 96-060291
ISBN 0-915024-50-0

Editor: Elizabeth McBride
Designer: Kathie Campbell
Editorial Intern: Erica Baumer
Milwaukee Chapter: Ann Christenson
Maps: Cartographic Solutions
Cover Photograph: Bayfield, B.W. Hoffmann

Printed in the United States of America by BookCrafters.

The publisher gratefully acknowledges local chambers of commerce, convention and visitors bureaus, businesses and historic sites for the use of photographs. The excerpt from *Wau-bun, The "Early Day" in the Northwest*, is reprinted with the permission of the National Society of the Colonial Dames of America in the State of Wisconsin.

Wisconsin Trails
P.O. Box 5650
Madison, WI 53705

CONTENTS

INTRODUCTION

W e love Wisconsin. Ours is a state so diverse in character that even we who know it well are continually awestruck. Charming villages, vast forests, rocky shores, golden cornfields, 15,000 perfect lakes—little wonder the Badger State is the Midwest's number-one vacation destination.

For more than 35 years, we have devoted our magazine, *Wisconsin Trails*, to celebrating this incredible place. In the process, we have visited more towns, hiked more trails, paddled more rivers, and driven more roads than we could ever count. And we have loved the journey. In this book we want to share some of these wonderful experiences with you.

From the most popular sections of our magazine, we have gathered here 14 of our favorite weekend destinations. Some are urban—like Milwaukee, our biggest, brashest city—others, rural. (In fact, towns don't come more rural than Rural, a tiny village in Waupaca County composed of 13 still-lived-in historic homes.) A few of our destinations are highly popular; many are "secrets" just too good to keep to ourselves. We've organized these weekend adventures by season so you will know the very best time to visit. We include maps and information on restaurants and lodging accommodations. And, so you won't run out of things to do, we suggest 80 other events and outings, our "top picks" for each season—driving tours, bicycling trails, candlelight hikes, museums, wildlife areas, even a smelt fry and a New Year's Day plunge in Lake Michigan (which you can just watch!).

We dedicate entire chapters to Madison and Milwaukee. Cities for all seasons, they contain enough diversions to keep you occupied all through the year. Then we wind up with a section on what our readers have told us are some of their favorite things: summer festivals. Imagine whole weekends devoted to art and folk music and sweet corn and bratwurt and chocolate and ... cow chips. Well, it boggles the mind.

Wisconsin is fun. And beautiful and friendly. We're sure, if you explore only a bit of what is described in this book, you will love it as much as we do. To avoid any disappointment, however, please call ahead before setting out to the places we mention. Though we have worked hard to ensure accuracy, establishments close and hours of operation and other details change over time.

We know there is lots more out there to explore. Write and tell us about your own discoveries. Our address is: Great Weekend Adventures, Wisconsin Trails, P.O. Box 5650, Madison, WI 53705.

Happy adventuring!

SPRING
flings

Spring is a restless time. Birds fly

overhead in great numbers toward

summer nesting grounds,

hibernating mammals shake off

their winter drowsiness to feed,

and fish thrash their way upstream

in spectacular spawning runs.

What a wonderful season to be

outside, to walk, fish and paddle,

to draw in the fragrant air,

and welcome back our green

and growing world.

PICKS OF THE SEASON

april, may & june

1 HIKING

WELCOME SPRING ON THE NORTH COUNTRY TRAIL

When completed, the North Country Trail will sweep 3,200 miles across the nation from Vermont to North Dakota. But, in a poetic sense, it really begins in Wisconsin. An existing 40-mile trail in Bayfield and Ashland counties inspired the National Park Service to create the longer route. It's easy to understand why. Hike Wisconsin's segment of the North Country Trail and you'll find quintessential "north country": brooks, bogs, forest and mountains,

Sandhill crane.

and so much solitude you'll want to walk forever. For information, contact the ranger districts at Glidden, (715) 264-2511; Hayward, (715) 634-4821; and Washburn, (715) 373-2667.

2 BIRDWATCHING

CREX MEADOWS, WATERFOWL PARADISE

Each spring, thousands of migrating geese, ducks, coots and cranes are drawn to the wetlands of the Crex Meadows Wildlife Area in Burnett County. The huge flocks of waterfowl are an incredible sight, and the dozens of bald eagles, scores of hawks and thousands of warblers and other birds only add to the spectacle.

The 30,000-acre wildlife area represents a prairie and marsh restoration project that began in 1946. About 80 percent of the land has been restored to its original brush prairie-wetland habitat, a landscape that was disturbed by drainage of the marsh by settlers in the 1890s.

You can hike through the area's oak and jack pine woods on two developed trails, or walk on miles of old roads that cross the prairie. You'll find Crex Meadows' headquarters eight miles north of Grantsburg. Call (715) 463-2899 for more information.

3 SHOPPING

EXPLORE HUDSON

When spring weather is just too harsh to handle, wander over to Hudson, a picturesque town tucked among the bluffs of the St. Croix River on Highway 35. Old brick buildings in the downtown historic district house antiques shops, art galleries and cafes. And the Third Street neighborhood, where lumber barons built their elaborate Victorian homes, is an architectural treasure. Be sure to stop by the cupola-topped Octagon House, one of the few eight-sided homes in the country open to the public. Call the Chamber of Commerce at (800) 657-6775 for a walking tour booklet.

4 WALKING

TO THE TOP OF TIMM'S HILL

Get your winter-creaky legs in shape with a walk to the state's highest point— Timm's Hill, in Price County. The summit rests 1,951.5 feet above sea level, with a panoramic view of the surrounding sugar maple forest. Timm's Hill County Park also contains two spring-fed lakes stocked with bass and pan fish, walking trails and a picnic shelter. It's located east of Ogema on Highway 86.

Long Slide Falls, Marinette County.

can be visited any time of year, but spring, when the streams are flooded with meltwater, is the most exciting waterfall season. Cascades can be found across the state's northern tier. Marinette County, which calls itself the Waterfall Capital of the World, has put together a map to help you find their falling waters. For a copy, call the county's tourism office at (800) 236-6681.

6 WALKING

CANDLELIGHT HIKE

Sometimes April is the cruelest month, delivering more of winter when our spirits yearn for spring. To soften the blow, the folks at Council Grounds State Park in Lincoln County schedule a candlelight walk in late April. Routes are either a half-mile or two and a half miles long. The Lions Club sells hot dogs, and two huge fireplaces ward off the chill. And if you miss the April hike, join one in another season—six to eight candlelight hikes a year are scheduled. Call (715) 536-4502 for exact dates and details.

5 DRIVING TOUR

THE WATERFALLS OF MARINETTE COUNTY

Falling water is electrifying: veils of mist rising, sun glinting on dancing droplets, a thrumming heartbeat that you feel as much as hear. Waterfalls

7 FISHING

WHERE THE TROUT ARE

With all the attention Wisconsin anglers shower on muskies and walleyes, some of the best trout fishing east of the Rockies tends to go unnoticed. And while trout streams embroider much of the northeast, the richest stitchery graces Langlade County. There's no more beautiful river in Wisconsin than the Wolf, alternately racing and purling through 50 miles of near wilderness. If you view it through a trout fisherman's eyes, it's doubly gorgeous: full of pools, pockets and riffles that beg to be explored with a fly, and wide enough to allow comfortable casting and wading. For up-to-the-minute conditions, call the Wolf River Fly Shop, (715) 882-5941.

Of course, even under the best conditions, fishing for wild trout is never a sure thing. If you're overcome by frustration—or if you just want to show the kids a good time— head for Silver Moon Springs on Highway 64 in Elton. The ponds are chock-full of fat brookies and rainbows that will literally fight over your lure. Call (715) 882-8176.

8 NATURE

SPAWNING SPECTACLE ON THE WOLF RIVER

A compelling spring show takes place each year in the cold waters of the Wolf River. In late April or early May, the sturgeon leave Lake Winnebago to swim 125 miles upriver to spawn. The fish wait in the middle of the river for up to a week until the tempera-

ture is right, then flail and splash upstream as the females drop their eggs and the males fertilize them. Seeing these huge, ancient fish—some 6 feet long—performing this timeless ritual is an unforgettable sight.

Fishing for trout.

A good viewing spot is the Shawano Dam a few blocks west of Highway 22 in Shawano. Another is about two miles west of New London on County X where the road parallels the riverbank. Or head west of Shiocton on Highway 54 and look for cars parked along the road. The DNR office in Green Bay (414-424-3050) can provide more information.

9 NATURE

ROAMING RIDGES SANCTUARY

If anyone thinks that the preservation vs. development struggle in Door County is a recent phenomenon, they need to be set straight. More than half a century ago, one of the most important environmental battles in the history of the peninsula was fought over 40 acres of low, sandy soil on the north shore of Baileys Harbor. The good guys won, and what might have been corrupted into a trailer park was given permanent protection. Today, the Ridges Sanctuary encompasses more than 1,200 acres, and is as ecologi-

Jacob Leinenkugel Brewing Co., Chippewa Falls.

cally precious a parcel as any in Door County—if not the entire state.

The ridges for which the sanctuary is named are a series of 29 curving, parallel beach ridges, separated by marshy swales, that mark the ancient Lake Michigan shorelines. This geological feature alone would warrant the area's preservation, but the Ridges is even wealthier in terms of its

botanical lode. The cool, moist microclimate created by the prevailing winds off Lake Michigan enables the growth of many plants normally found much farther north. Some 28 species of native orchids thrive in this unique environment, including the secretive ram's head and pink lady's-slipper; 13 plants considered endangered or threatened in Wisconsin also prosper here.

You can take a self-guided tour of the Ridges, or sign up for a walk led by a staff naturalist. For details, call (414) 839-2802. The sanctuary is located on County Q outside Baileys Harbor.

10 BREWERY TOUR

AN INSIDE LOOK AT LEINENKUGEL'S

Microbrewing and specialty beers are hot trends in the brewing industry. But that's old news to the people of Chippewa Falls. More than 125 years ago, German immigrant Jacob Leinenkugel built his brewery here, in what was then a logging town of 2,500 (mostly male) residents. Since then, the brewery has thrived with five generations of Leinenkugels at the helm. (Miller Brewing Co. bought the brewery in 1988, but the Leinenkugel family still oversees day-to-day operations.)

The distinctive beer is still produced in the original kettles in the original buildings. Tours of the operation are offered Monday through Friday from September through May, and Monday through Saturday in June, July and August. Call (715) 723-5557 for reservations.

11 OPEN HOUSE

DRIVING FORT McCOY

Well-known for its military re-enactments and equipment displays, Fort McCoy offers visitors a nature experience as well. Positioned on 60,000 acres in Monroe County, the fort is a wildlife haven. Back roads pass through a rough course full of pine and deer, where signs caution tank crossings. Resplendent views of the distant blue hills and valleys deep in the interior's restricted zone might have the added dimension of a parachute-diving practice.

The fort, dating to the turn of the century, housed a Civilian Conservation Corps camp during the Great Depression. Today National Guard units practice maneuvers on weekends. A special day for the public, the Armed Forces Open House, is scheduled during May. Events include a World War II re-enactment and displays of military equipment. For more information and/or a map of the 23-mile driving tour, contact the Fort McCoy Public Affairs Office at (608) 388-2407.

Fort McCoy, Monroe County.

12 CANOEING

THE WINDING KICKAPOO

From the town of Ontario, south of the dam, the Kickapoo River snakes through some of the wildest, most verdant land of Vernon County, attracting herons, muskrats, deer and canoeists. The water skirts the edges of hillsides and occasional cliffs that loom overhead crowned with hemlock and pine. The deep shadows and high banks create a canyon effect, and the steady current gives respite from continual paddling. Intriguing bends and turns are a matter of course.

A favorite day trip starts at bridge #1 in Ontario and continues to the remains of bridge #12 just south of Rockton. A good two-day trip continues to La Farge. For more details and for information on canoe rentals, call (608) 337-4711.

13 NATURE
COUNTING CRANES

Every April, close to 3,000 people around the state gather in wetlands not yet fully released from winter's grasp to catch a glimpse or hear the wild trumpeting call of a sandhill crane. The Annual Midwest Sandhill Crane Count, organized by the International Crane Foundation in Baraboo, tallies the frequency and distribution of these magnificent birds. A volunteer effort, it is one of the largest single-species surveys in the world.

The count is an educational tool, as well. Out in a marsh at 5:30 a.m., participants spot not only cranes but red-winged blackbirds, warblers, deer,

Sandhill crane.

beaver and migrating ducks. Notes Crane Count coordinator Rob Nelson, "That sharpens their observation skills and gives them a deeper appreciation for the ecosystem."

Though not everyone spots cranes, the odds are good. Volunteers generally see or hear between 6,000 and 12,000 birds, a remarkable increase from the 25 pairs the population was reduced to in the early part of this century. If you would like to participate, call (608) 356-9462.

14 NATURE
STOP AND SMELL THE LILACS

When one of the country's largest collection of lilacs reaches full bloom, the UW-Madison Arboretum in Madison is a heady place to visit. The lilacs are concentrated in the 50-acre Longenecker Gardens, near the Arboretum's visitor center, and invite strolling, lounging and, of course, sniffing. The 1,200-acre retreat contains plenty of walking trails as well, through hardwood and pine forests and the world's oldest restored tallgrass prairie. For a trail map, call (608) 263-7888.

15 HORSE SHOW
THESE CLYDES ARE FOR YOU

It's impossible to realize how big a Clydesdale (the Budweiser horse) is until you stand

Judy Larson and two of her famous Clydesdales.

next to one. The statistics are impressive: birth weight, 250 pounds; adult weight more than 2,000 pounds; and full height over 6 feet tall at the withers. But those numbers don't have much meaning until a huge, white-blazed head reaches down to greet you or you see a handler having to stand on a 6-foot stepladder to braid a mane. Then you realize "huge" has a whole new definition.

You can meet some Clydesdales face-to-face (face-to-withers?) at Larson's Famous Clydesdales in Ripon, a full-scale breeding operation and home of national six-hitch champions. Visitors can observe the horses being harnessed; see the wagons, trucks, trailers and equipment necessary for showing; and watch six Clydes perform intricate driving maneuvers. The Larsons also have a Clydesdale souvenir shop and museum on the grounds. Shows and tours are offered May through October. A special treat in spring: the chance to pet a 300-pound baby Clydesdale. Call (414) 748-5466 for hours.

16 MUSEUM
WHAT A CIRCUS

Baraboo was the hub of the Ringling brothers' circus for 34 years, between 1884 and 1918 when this sleepy Sauk County town served as winter quarters. Today, Circus World Museum occupies many of the original Ringling buildings—all historic landmarks. Owned by the State Historical Society, it is the world's largest museum devoted to circus life.

But this is no dusty, musty warehouse. The exhibit halls are crowded with fascinating circus curios, from tiny flea circus paraphernalia to the huge human cannon used by Frank "Fearless" Gregg in 1930. A football-field-size building houses a dazzling collection of elaborately carved circus parade wagons. And from May to September, the museum treats visitors to a full-fledged circus of its own in an outdoor tent, with high-wire artists, performing pachyderms, equestrians, jugglers and clowns.

The museum is located at 426 Water St. in Baraboo. For hours and admission fees, call (608) 356-0800 or 356-8341.

17 NATURE
AT THE SUGARBUSH

When the snow finally melted and the "maple moon" rose, Native Americans knew it was time for maple sugaring. Using a spile made of staghorn sumac, they tapped dozens, sometimes hundreds, of sugar maple trees for sap,

Circus World Museum clown.

9

then boiled the sap down to a thick, sweet syrup. The Indians taught the process to pioneers; today's maple syrup producers, with a few changes in equipment, follow the same method.

Riveredge Nature Center, near Newburg, invites you to their 30-acre sugar bush in late March and early April, where you can follow a self-guided trail to learn more about sugarin' and watch syrup being made. On the last day of the process, organizers serve up all the pancakes you can eat, right in the bush, within sniffing distance of the boiling sweet stuff. For details, call (414) 675-6888.

18 EVENT

FISH, CHIPS & FUN

Every spring, fried-fish connoisseurs converge on the Lake Michigan city of Port Washington—and they never go home hungry. The attraction? Smelt. For the past 30-odd years, folks have gathered here the first weekend after Easter for the World's Largest Smelt Fry. Over the course of it, a ton of deep-fried smelt is served. If you're not up on your fish, smelt are small, minnow-sized fish, and, as Bruce Wenzel, bartender at the American Legion Hall where the smelt fry is held, says, "You eat the bones and everything. But you don't even notice it." For information, call (414) 284-4690.

19 SPORTS SHOW

GET READY— SUMMER'S COMING!

March is a great time for dreaming of adventure. Attend one of the sport and travel shows happening this month, and you'll be ready to make the most of the first warm day of spring.

The biggest is the Milwaukee Sentinal Sports Show, with 500 exhibits geared for every outdoor enthusiast. Among a host of activities, you can pick up tips on rock climbing, view the newest line of boats, watch a lumberjack show, and listen to presentations by a wide range of nationally known outdoorspeople. Those interested in quieter pursuits may learn how to build a bird house, identify edible plants, or cast a line into a trout stream right on the premises. The show is held at MECCA, at the corner of Fourth Street and Kilbourn Avenue, and runs mid-March. For exact dates and advance tickets, call (800) 876-3320.

The state's other big sport show is the Northeast Wisconsin Sport Fishing Show held in late March at the Brown County Arena in Green Bay. For more information, call (800) 628-7971.

weekend ADVENTURES

Savor Wisconsin's premier destinations— Door County and Wisconsin Dells—when they are blissfully uncrowded. Then step off the beaten track into Portage, one of our most historic towns.

JACKSONPORT

WISCONSIN DELLS

PORTAGE

Jacksonport, Unspoiled Door County

Jacksonport is where the geographical features that define Wisconsin—farmland, forest and water—intersect. Approaching this quiet, seemly village from the south, as visitors are bound to do, the open countryside invites the eye to roam. There are mellow pastures here, bright-green orchards and fields of sturdy corn. Then, as the road curves, gently descending into the village, the view is suddenly constricted by ranks of solemn, magisterial pines. It is as if a line has been crossed, a line that divides the arable realm from the great North Woods. Curiously—or perhaps cosmographically—this division falls within a mile or so of the 45th meridian, the halfway point between the equator and the North Pole.

Of course, Jacksonport's proximity to Lake Michigan

Quiet beauty beckons near Jacksonport.

makes it feel as if it's considerably closer to the pole than it is. This vast sea surges at the village's doorstep, and its moods determine everything, from the smelt run to the apple harvest to the turnout for the Maifest parade. It is the reason that spring is fleeting, autumn elongated, and summer deliciously cool.

THE VILLAGE

Long before Andrew Jackson (no relation to "Old Hickory") financed a massive logging operation in what was then a wilderness, people were drawn to the area that has since borne his name. The banks of Heins and Hibbard creeks were occupied by intermittent Indian encampments for several hundred years—fish and game were plentiful, and corn could be grown in the sandy soil. By the time Jackson and his crew arrived around the middle of the 19th century, however, the native peoples had already departed, largely because of intertribal warring. Legend has it that much of the lumber used to rebuild Chicago after its cataclysmic fire came from Jacksonport and thereabouts. True or not, the big timber was cut, and Jacksonport evolved into a pleasant little community of farmers, orchardists and fishermen.

Which it still is. The village has, so far, escaped the ram-

pant commercialization that has afflicted other parts of Door County. As a result, Jacksonport has retained its friendly, serene, unhurried character, its unforced charm. Is this the way Door County used to be? Maybe. Is this the way Door County was meant to be? Absolutely.

Jacksonport contains no

Cave Point County Park.

hidden corners; what you see is pretty much what you get. Highway 57 bisects the village longitudinally. Homes, cottages and business establishments—none grand or pretentious in the least—flank it on both sides.

A tour of Jacksonport begins at its south end with a stop at the Meunier Studio Gallery. The nostalgic red brick schoolhouse is now the studio of pianist-composer Dan Meunier, whose original recordings interpret the seasons and the spirit of Door County with sensitivity and panache. (That's Dan's music you hear playing in shops and restaurants throughout the Door). Pick up his albums here, or catch one of his weekend summer concerts; call ahead for a schedule (414-823-2044).

Farther up Highway 57, the Jacksonport Craft Cottage, an 1867 structure built by Andrew Jackson as a lumbering office and living quarters, features the work of 60 artists, including Amish quilts, pottery and handmade dolls. La Mere House Antiques sells exquisite showpieces in antique walnut, rosewood, satinwood, cherry, oak, bird's-eye maple, mahogany and pine in an 1860s home. At the north end of the village, check out The Collector's Antiques, which is literally bursting at the seams with fondly remembered stuff.

If you're looking for an uncrowded beach on a sunny, summer afternoon, look no farther than Lakeside Park. With grills, tables, swings and even restrooms (very important), it's a great place for family picnics. Though no one has yet solved the sticky problem of how to successfully take ice cream to the beach, fear not. You can get good cones at the Porthole, right next to the park. Any other necessities can be picked up at Vi's Grocery, an institution in Jacksonport since 1960. Vi herself (Viola Tanck), one of the kindest,

warmest, most delightful people you'll ever meet, personifies all that is best about Jacksonport. She and butcher Wayne Bley make bratwurst, *sulz* (a pungent headcheese) and a variety of other wondrous sausages that are (pardon the pun) to Vi for.

Across the street from Vi's is LeClair's Fish Market, where you can always purchase whitefish fresh from the cold, clear depths of Lake Michigan and, from time to time, smoked whitefish and chubs as well. (Insider's tip: To buy fish, go to the north side of the building. The east side—on the highway—is where the laundromat is.)

You'll want to familiarize yourself as well with Town Hall Bakery, from whose ovens emerge pecan rolls that are out of this world. The bakery's oatmeal-cherry cookies—made, of course, with real Door County cherries—are another favorite; plan on buying a bagful for the road.

THE TOWNSHIP

Determining where the village of Jacksonport ends and the township of the same name begins is a by-gosh-and-by-golly kind of deal. "Where the houses stop" seems as accurate a reckoning as any, although there are small enclaves scattered at random across the rolling, alternately tilled and wooded countryside.

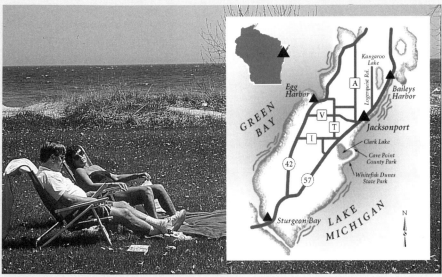

Relaxation at an uncrowded beach.

EATING WELL

Square Rigger Galley—In the heart of Jacksonport, Square Rigger serves traditional Door County fish boils nightly during the summer—and does it, fittingly, within a stone's throw of Lake Michigan. The restaurant's breakfasts are excellent too. (414) 823-2408.

Mr. G's—Featuring steaks, prime rib and seafood (and, they say, the best broiled whitefish in Door County), Mr. G's has the rustic ambiance of a classic North Woods supper club. South of town on Highway 57. (414) 823-2112.

Voight's Lakeside Inn—Excellent steaks, fish and poultry served in a friendly, relaxed ambiance. Nightly specials; hearty lunches, too. Open May 1 through the last Saturday in October. Corner of Highway 57 and County V. (414) 823-2542.

Mike's Port Pub—Besides cooking up great "bar" food—burgers, chili, assorted hot munchies—Mike's, located right in Jackson-

port, serves one of the best Friday night perch fries north of Green Bay. While it might not be the case that everybody knows your name at Mike's, it's still as cheerful a watering hole as you'll find on the Door. (414) 823-2081.

LODGING

Square Rigger Lodge—In the heart of downtown Jacksonport (if there is such a thing), this clean, comfortable, modern motel comes complete with sauna, whirlpool, sand beach and a glorious view of Lake Michigan. For those wanting a little more space and privacy, the Square Rigger also rents five housekeeping cottages. (414) 823-2404.

Carolyn's Cottages—On Clark Lake, two-bedroom cottages offer affordable lakefront seclusion and beautiful sunsets. (414) 823-2222.

The Rushes—This luxurious condominium development on Kangaroo Lake features a swimming beach, tennis courts, indoor swimming pool, whirlpool and steamroom. (414) 839-2730.

Whitefish Bay Farm Bed & Breakfast—For those who prefer countryside to waterfront, this restored 1908 farmhouse sits just up the road from Whitefish Dunes. (414) 743-1560.

SPRING EVENTS

Maifest—Held Memorial Day weekend, Maifest kicks off the Door County "season" with a parade, carnival, arts and crafts fair, dancing, food (from fish boil to funnel cakes) and sheer unrelieved merrymaking.

IN OTHER SEASONS

Northeastern Wisconsin Antique Power Association Thresheree—Dozens of old-time tractors, steam engines, saws and other amazing contraptions are on display at the Geisel farm in nearby Valmy. Usually held late August, the thresheree is the kind of event that children should take their grandparents to.
For more information, contact the Door County Chamber, (414) 743-4456.

PEOPLE OF THE DUNES

Centuries before Jean Nicolet gazed upon the limestone bluffs and wave-lapped beaches of the Door Peninsula, Native American civilizations flourished here. And nowhere did these civilizations find the hunting, fishing and living more to their liking than in the area of what is now Jacksonport. Digs at Whitefish Dunes State Park have unearthed archeological evidence of eight separate occupations. The earliest, by a culture known as the North Bay People, dates to 100 B.C. The nature center at the state park (south of Jacksonport on Cave Point Road) includes a display of artifacts, and there's a free descriptive brochure, "People of the Dunes," that is well worth reading.

The banks of Heins and Hibbard creeks were also attractive to Wisconsin's indigenous cultures. The Potawatomi believed that their ancestors had inhabited the Hibbard Creek site for some 600 years; at its peak in the mid-17th century, the village—a city, really—may have supported as many as 3,000 people. It was called "Mechingan" (Michigan) then, although the Jesuit missionaries, who began making contact at about this time, were hopeful of changing its name to St. Michael.

Sadly, no trace of this site remains. As H.R. Holand wrote in 1917 in his *History of Door County, Wisconsin*: "For years this place has been a mecca for Indian relic hunters. ... Every strong wind from the east would expose the skeletons of Indians buried there, rings, beads and ornaments of copper, silver and bone, which the boys of the vicinity would gather." The wind still blows, but the sands of Jacksonport have no more secrets to reveal.

Whitefish Dunes State Park.

West Jacksonport, at the intersection of county highways V and T is such a place, a rural crossroads whose claim to fame is a baseball diamond that could have served as the model for the one in *Field of Dreams*. Hit a hanging curve over the fence, and the horsehide lands in the corn. Game time is Sunday afternoon.

Speaking of horsehide, Kurtz Corral (County I south of Jacksonport) offers trail rides for equestrians of all ages and abilities, as well as English and western lessons by reservation.

Bicycling is excellent on Jacksonport's lightly traveled byways. For particularly scenic pedaling, take Cave Point Road south around Clark Lake to Loritz Road. Follow Loritz north, jogging west on County V to continue north on County T. Head east on Junction Road and south on County A to complete a 15-mile loop.

Door County's largest inland lakes, Clark and Kangaroo, attract quiet-water canoeists, small-boat sailors and a cadre of windsurfers, not to mention anglers lured by the promise of walleye, bass and pan fish. On moonlit spring nights, Heins and Hibbard creeks are hotspots for smelt. Big, hard-fighting steelhead hold in these streams too, posing a terrific challenge to even the most accomplished trout angler. Trout—brookies mostly—can also be found among the watercress in Logan Creek, part of which meanders through the Logan Creek Property, a 140-acre tract of mixed timber (including some immense virgin hemlocks) owned and managed by the Ridges Sanctuary in nearby Baileys Harbor.

On a more consumptive note, the Bright Eye Farm Market on Highway 57 south of the village sells organically grown vegetables of impeccable freshness and flavor, along with other healthy, tasty produce. Food for the eyes awaits at Ironwood Metalsmithing, 3435 Junction Road, where Dick and Barbara Kolpack forge spectacular lawn sculptures and elegant wrought-iron furnishings for the home. Located in a restored barn, the Fieldstone Gallery, on Logerquist Road north of Highway 57, houses an eclectic collection that ranges from jewelry, pottery and prints to Amish bentwood rockers. Jacksonport watercolorist Kari Anderson, unfortunately, doesn't have her own gallery, but it's worth the drive to Ephraim for her evocative, often whimsical prints, posters and cards.

IN THE AREA

No trip to Jacksonport—indeed to Door County—would be complete without a stop at Cave Point County Park, on Cave Point Road south of Jacksonport. The sight of the relentless Lake Michigan surf crashing into those stern headlands, and the thunderous sound of its impact, inspire a kind of ancient, elemental awe. On calm days, anglers casting spoons from the ledges there have been known to catch enormous brown trout.

Literally surrounding Cave Point and extending for more than a mile down the shoreline is Whitefish Dunes State Park. It boasts the highest sand dunes on the Wisconsin side of Lake Michigan and the most popular swimming beaches in the state. A network of hiking trails winds inland, trails on which you are as likely to encounter browsing deer as other people. The park staff offers regularly scheduled nature programs throughout the summer. ■

THE DELLS

Visit the Serene Side of the Dells

Fifteen thousand years ago, at the end of the last Ice Age, glacial meltwater streamed through the soft sandstone gorge of the Wisconsin Dells. The water cut deep canyons, draped with ferns and hemlocks, and from ancient rock, part-hard and part-soft, it carved incredible formations that stood along the banks of the river like guardian spirits. For generations, Native Americans camped here, believing the Dells to be sacred. Then, in the 1860s, tourists arrived to view the peculiar rock outcroppings. Local businesses sought to keep these tourists entertained for weekend and, eventually, weeklong vacations, and over the years the town of Wisconsin Dells became famous for its manmade adventures—theme parks, waterslides, mini-golf courses and other family attractions. But the Dells' rich heritage and

Lift-off at the Great Wisconsin Dells Balloon Rally.

breathtaking natural beauty remain intact, and are just as captivating today as when the first tourists arrived here more than a century ago.

THE LAND

Photographer H.H. Bennett, more than any other individual, was responsible for introducing the world to Wisconsin Dells' striking landscape. Bennett came to what was then called Kilbourn City with his father in 1857 and worked as a carpenter. After his right hand was permanently injured in the Civil War, he purchased a portrait studio and taught himself photography. Bennett could not confine himself to portraits, however, instead becoming one of the first photojournalists, capturing on film the last lumber run through the Dells' treacherous waters. And he explored, almost unceasingly, the canyons of the Dells themselves.

Riding a wave of public interest in stereography, Bennett sold scenic views. When an enterprising pilot began rowing visitors upriver, he photographed their expeditions as well. In effect, Bennett marketed the Dells as gentle, serene and accessible to the general public, and in the mid-1870s, when steam-powered excursion boats were introduced, people came in droves.

A guided cruise is the best way to view what so powerfully lured these 19th-century tourists. The cliffs are not quite as tall as they once were; because of modern-day dams the water level in the Wisconsin River has risen about 20 feet. But very little else has changed. In the late 19th century, Bennett's daughter and her

Scale model of H.H. Bennett Studio.

husband purchased hundreds of acres of shoreline property to prevent development; their daughters transferred it to the Wisconsin Alumni Research Foundation, which has kept this strip of land singularly unspoiled. The Department of Natural Resources acquired the property in 1993, and is drafting plans to manage it as a natural area.

The Upper Dells tour, a two-hour ride, leads to the most rugged scenery. Blue-and-white double-decker boats, built in the 1950s, drift past 70-foot-tall cliffs, striped with buff, gold and grey rock—Cambrian sandstone, formed 500 million years ago and found exposed in only two other areas of the world. Nineteenth-century tourists looked for familiar images in the castellated rock, and tour boat operators still point out Chief Black Hawk's profile, an alligator, toadstool and other such images.

At Devil's Elbow, named by lumbermen who struggled to steer huge log rafts through its bend, lacy cedar branches veil the river. At Witches Gulch, riders debark and follow a boardwalk into a spectacular side canyon. Bennett discovered Witches Gulch in the 1870s by ice-skating into the gorge and climbing up the frozen waterfall. In 1875, he and his brothers built a walk-way, and the gulch has been a favored tourist spot ever since. One of the Dells' most memorable features, it's cool and dim even on the hottest summer days. Moss clings to the damp walls. A stream of water gurgles below the walkway, swirls through whirlpool chambers, then plunges into a deep pool. High above, one can just glimpse hemlocks and white pines against a blue sky.

The one-hour, nonstop Lower Dells tour cruises past the Rocky Islands and areas of the river that figured prominently in the region's logging history. Contact Dells Boat Tours (608-253-1561, 254-8500, 254-8336) for information on both the Upper and Lower Dells tours.

You can also explore the Dells by canoe, but because of the high level of recreational boat traffic on the river, you might want to restrict your paddling to spring or fall. Rentals are available at Point Bluff Resort, (608) 253-6181; Lake Delton Water Sports, (608) 254-8702; and Holiday Shores Water Sports, (608) 254-2878. A tranquil experience is guaranteed any time of the year if you choose to sight-see via hot-air balloon. Elusive Dream Balloons, (608) 586-5737, will lift you up at sunrise or sunset for an unforgettable birds-eye view of the Wisconsin River's graceful curves and soaring sandstone cliffs. For a closer look at land and sea, take a ride on one of the Original Wisconsin Ducks, amphibious war vehicles that journey down the river and along fernlined wilderness trails to a restored prairie (608-254-8751).

In town, the H.H. Bennett Museum at 215 Broadway (608-253-2261) is packed tight with the photographers' stun-

EATING WELL

The Cheese Factory—An alternative to standard supper-club fare, this restaurant specializes in international vegetarian cuisine, such as pizza with Brie and calamata olives, tapas and Thai stir-fries. Order a thick milkshake or cherry Coke from the soda fountain. 521 Wisconsin Dells Parkway. (608) 253-6065.

Wally's House of Embers—A Dells landmark, Wally's House of Embers serves hickory-smoked barbecued ribs, Austrian veal and fresh salmon. 935 Wisconsin Dells Parkway. (608) 253-6411.

Del-Bar Supper Club—Established in 1943, Del-Bar is famous for its certified Black Angus steaks. 800 Wisconsin Dells Parkway. (608) 253-1861.

Thunder Valley Inn—May to October, this inn serves Scandinavian-style breakfasts daily, Friday-night fish fries and Saturday threshing suppers with "food and entertainment as it once was." Reservations required for the Saturday night threshing supper. W15344 Waubeek Rd. (608) 254-4145.

Dells Grill—Only in the Dells could a small cafe with clanking dishes and a sizzling grill seem peaceful. Refreshingly old-fashioned, Dells Grill serves juicy burgers with fried onions, homemade coleslaw and thick slabs of Dutch apple pie. 324 Broadway. (608) 254-2727.

LODGING

Historic Bennett House Bed & Breakfast—The former home of photographer H.H. Bennett contains three elegant guest rooms and features antiques, tall windows and Bennett's own bathtub. Proprietors Gail and Rich Obermeyer can provide a wealth of information on the region and

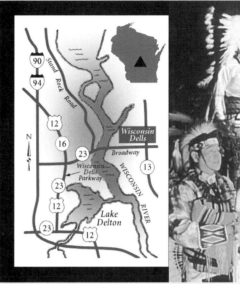

Indian Ceremonial at Stand Rock.

its history. (608) 254-2500.

Seth Peterson Cottage—On the edge of Mirror Lake State Park, this is the only Frank Lloyd Wright-built home you can rent. Make reservations early. (608) 254-6551.

Camping—Available at Rocky Arbor State Park (608-254-8001) and Mirror Lake State Park (608-254-2333). Both include handicapped facilities.

Motels, resorts, cabins and private campgrounds—Contact Wisconsin Dells Visitor & Convention Bureau, 701 Superior St., Wisconsin Dells, WI 53965; (800) 22-DELLS.

SPRING EVENTS

Great Wisconsin Dells Balloon Rally—Ninety hot-air balloons create a colorful spectacle in early June (the weekend after Memorial Day weekend) as they lift off from a field near the intersection of I-90/94 and Highway 12. Ascents, weather permitting, are Saturday, 6:30 a.m. and 6 p.m., and Sunday, 6:30 a.m.

Heritage Day Celebration—An arts and crafts fair, pancake breakfast, ice-cream social, quilt show and tours of the home of Jonathan Bowman, one of the town's prominent early residents, are scheduled. Held in early June.

IN OTHER SEASONS

Polish-American Fest—Traditional Polish dress, food, music and dance are featured. Held the first weekend following Labor Day.

Wo-Zha-Wa Days Fall Festival—Autumn celebration with arts and crafts, antiques and entertainment. Held the second weekend after Labor Day.

Wisconsin Dells Polka Fest—Polka bash held in early November.

Flake Out Festival—Snow-sculpting, ice carving, horse-drawn sleigh rides, music, food and a hot-air balloon lift-off, scheduled for the third weekend in January. *For more information, contact Wisconsin Dells Visitor & Convention Bureau, (800) 22-DELLS.*

ning black-and-white images. The studio, on the National Register of Historic Places and still owned by the Bennett family, contains its original furnishings and much of Bennett's equipment. Besides viewing prints made by Bennett himself, you can purchase new prints created from original glass-plate negatives, along with stereoscopic views. For a glimpse of the Dells' railway history, stop by the Amtrack station, 100 La Crosse St., which was rebuilt by volunteers in the 1980s in the style of the 1880s Kilbourn Depot. Inside, you'll find historic photos and artifacts, including the depot's original wooden benches. The station is open when trains come through: 11:30 a.m. to 12:30 p.m. and 6 to 7 p.m.

The Dells was a sacred place to Native Americans, and their presence remains strong. The Ho-Chunk (formerly called Winnebago) were removed from their land here by the treaty of 1837 and sent to reservations out West. However, a band led by Chief Yellow Thunder, who considered the treaty to be a fraud, returned to Wisconsin in 1841. A few years later, Yellow Thunder purchased 40 acres in the Dells, and in the succeeding decades he lobbied Congress to allow the Ho-Chunk to buy homestead properties so they could always remain in

the area.

Today, the Indian Ceremonial at Stand Rock is the most dramatic display of Dells Indian culture. Begun in 1929, it includes speeches, songs and traditional dancing accompanied by the haunting sounds of drums, rattles and flutes. Though the ceremonial is now a commercial operation, the Ho-Chunk point out that the natural amphitheater in which it is held was always a special place for the tribe and that the ceremonial itself is an outgrowth of gatherings held there to honor Chief Yellow Thunder. Performances are scheduled nightly mid-June to Labor Day. Call (608) 253-7444 for ticket information.

At the junction of River Road and Highway 13, you'll find the Winnebago Indian Museum, begun by Roger (Little Eagle) Tallmadge in 1953. Tallmadge was a Minnesota Sioux who became a local tourism leader after moving to the Dells. His small museum with hand-lettered signs, now run by his wife and daughter, displays points, arrowheads and pottery shards that Tallmadge found in the area, 19th-century Sioux clothing and a wonderful collection of beaded moccasins. A shop sells handwoven Ho-Chunk baskets and silver jewelry.

Downtown in the Parkway Mall on Highway 12, Lance Tallmadge (Roger's son) operates Little Eagle Trading Company, a new shop selling a wide assortment of Native American items, including locally made baskets, Chippewa porcupine-quill boxes, paintings, books, tapes and jewelry. You can also purchase Ho-Chunk baskets and view Indian artifacts at Parson's Indian Trading Post and Museum on Highway 12.

IN THE AREA

Just north of town on Highway 12 lies Rocky Arbor State Park, a kind of mini-Dells and a real gem. Picnic here under the red pines or walk a one-mile nature trail, skirting a 500-million-year-old sandstone ledge before climbing into a dense maple woods.

Mirror Lake State Park, south of the Dells on Ferndell Road, offers equally enjoyable terrain, with sandstone bluffs sheltering a quiet lake, 20 miles of hiking trails and, in the spring, pink and yellow ladys-slipper orchids.

Also south of the Dells on Shady Lane Road, the International Crane Foundation harbors all the crane species of the world. Guided tours of the grounds, which include displays, slide programs and a restored prairie, are offered daily from Memorial Day through Labor Day. Tours are given on weekends throughout the season. Call (608) 356-9462 for more information. ■

Lumber rafts once filled these waters.

RAFTING OVER

Even before tourists came to Wisconsin Dells, it was frequently crowded—with lumbermen. In the latter part of the 19th century, the height of the lumbering era, lumbermen floated a million board feet a year down the Wisconsin River. In the area of the Dells, they had to navigate two of the most dangerous spots on the entire river: the right-angle turn in the Narrows, called the Devil's Elbow, and the dam at Kilbourn (now the town of Wisconsin Dells). To get through, rafts of sawn lumber would have to be split into sections. Often an entire crew was needed to wrestle each section over the dam; the crew would then walk 10 miles back up the riverbank to the head of the Dells to take another down. When the river was flooding, lumbermen tied up big fleets of rafts at the head of the Dells and waited for the water to drop to a safe level. Kilbourn, as Wisconsin Dells was then called, was a lively place when the rafting crews were in town. Because it was the scene of so much boisterous activity, one section of Superior Street was nicknamed "Bloody Run." Look for a historical marker at the tour boat dock, which indicates the spot below the dam where lumbermen reassembled their rafts.

PORTAGE

Historic Portage

The Ho-Chunk Indians called it "Wau-wau-o-nah," which meant the place between the Fox and Wisconsin rivers where one shouldered a canoe. The French descriptive, "le portage," is the one that stuck. By any name, this mile and a half stretch of land was of great significance; using this connection, explorers and trappers could travel by water all the way from the East Coast to the Gulf of Mexico. In 1828, the U.S. infantry built a fort here to protect the fur trade. Fifty years later, a canal was cut to facilitate commerce. The railroad laid its tracks, too, at what was then the edge of the northern pinery, and hauled lumber from this important switching post to big cities south and east.

Art show at Pauquette Park.

Perhaps it was because of this remarkable location, or simply a twist of fate, that Portage became a birthing ground for greatness. Frontier historian Frederick Jackson Turner, one of the most influential scholars of the 20th century, grew up here. Pioneering conservationist John Muir lived his formative teenage years on a farm in the nearby countryside. Aldo Leopold's Sand County shack stood just across the river. And in 1921, native Zona Gale, who made her reputation writing about her "Friendship Village," became the first woman to win the Pulitzer Prize for drama.

Visit Portage now and you'll find yourself steeped in history, and surrounded by a pastoral landscape that still offers tranquillity and inspiration.

THE CITY

One of the most remarkable features of Portage is that, in an era when the male point of view dominated, its early history was recorded by a woman. Juliette Magill, born into New England society, married Indian agent John Kinzie and traveled to the frontier in 1830 on her wedding trip, sometimes sleeping on a mattress atop her piano, which was balanced in a boat. Juliette Kinzie embraced pioneer life with enthusiasm and good cheer, and her book,

Old Indian Agency House.

Wau-bun, is a fascinating account of her experiences on the land that would become the city of Portage.

The Kinzie home, the Old Indian Agency House, stands near the site of Fort Winnebago under the shade of a 200-year-old elm. It should be the first stop on a visit to the area.

25

Although most of the family's furnishings were destroyed in the great Chicago fire of 1871 (after the Kinzies left Portage in 1833, John became Chicago's first village president), the Colonial Dames of Wisconsin have restored the house with fine antiques of the period, including a Sheraton sideboard and Hitchcock chairs. Thanks to Juliette's book, guides are able to relate detailed stories about the Kinzies and their compassionate dealings with the Ho-Chunk, who at the time were being removed from their land.

Tours are also offered of the nearby Surgeon's Quarters. The only remaining building of Fort Winnebago, it's filled with exhibits, military uniforms, household items and other artifacts. The one-room Garrison School next door, in use from 1850 to 1960 and furnished with double desks and period textbooks, is also open to the public. A historical marker across the road notes the site where explorers Marquette and Joliet crossed the portage in 1673.

The Portage Canal, one of only two canals built in Wisconsin before railroads made them obsolete, runs nearby. You can see this waterway by following a section of the Ice Age Trail that starts down the road from the Indian Agency House. (Be prepared to push through some brush.) Or enjoy a free canoe ride during Canal Days held annually in early June.

For a self-guided drive or walk around the city itself, pick up a brochure at the Information Center at the intersection of West Wisconsin (Highway 33) and West Cook streets (Highway 16). You'll find Society Hill dotted with handsome, Victorian mansions built of Portage cream brick, with carriage houses still standing alongside them. Pauquette Park, designed by Frederick Law Olmstead—who also created New York's Central Park—is a delightful oasis, with a lagoon, two bridges and, in summer, a smattering of kids fishing to the drone of cicadas.

Zona Gale's home stands at 506 W. Edgewater. Once called the most intensely American writer of her time, Gale was born in Portage in 1874. She worked as a reporter for the *Milwaukee Journal* and New York's *Evening World*, then turned her attention to writing romantic stories for leading magazines; Gale went on to write more than 30 books and plays. She returned to Portage in 1911, where she was a social and political figure, identifying herself with progressivism, prohibition, women's rights and international peace. After her death, her husband, William Breese, donated two of her houses to the people of Portage. The Greek Revival building on West Edgewater, in

Surgeon's Quarters on the site of Fort Winnebago.

EATING WELL

Hitching Post—Steaks, broasted chicken and seafood specials draw locals to this popular eatery. 2503 W. Wisconsin St. (608) 742-8208.

The Saloon—Build your own sandwich or indulge in tacos and burritos. 123 E. Cook St. (608) 742-2277.

Blankenhaus—The family-owned supper club, open Tuesday through Sunday, features an all-you-can-eat barbecue and seafood buffet on Wednesday nights, and an all-you-can-eat Sunday brunch. 1223 E. Wisconsin. (608) 742-7555.

The Sandhill Inn—South of Portage in Merrimac, the Sandhill Inn presents gourmet fare in an elegant Victorian home. Open for dinner Tuesday through Saturday, 5:30 to 10:30 p.m., and for Sunday

brunch, 9:30 a.m. to 2 p.m. Reservations requested. Highway 78. (608) 493-2203.

LODGING

The Riverbend Inn—The restored farmhouse outside Portage contains a luxury suite and three guest rooms. (608) 742-3627.

Neenah Creek Inn and Pottery—The turn-of-the-century cream brick house, 15 miles northwest of Portage in Endeavor, is situated on 11 country acres with gardens and walking paths. The host is a potter, who gives demonstrations of his craft upon request. (608) 587-2229.

Hotels and motels—Numerous additional accommodations are available in Wisconsin Dells, 13 miles west of Portage. Call the Wisconsin Dells Visitor & Convention Bureau at (800) 22-DELLS for information.

SPRING EVENTS

Canal Days—Town celebration with parade, carnival, flea market, buckskinner rendezvous, reduced admission at historic sites and, on Saturday, races and free canoe rides on the canal. Usually held the first weekend in June.

IN OTHER SEASONS

Friendship Village Celebrates Zona Gale—Commemoration in August of the writer's life includes graveside eulogies, play and poetry readings, speeches and guided tours of Gale's home.

Taste of Portage—Local venders sell samples of their fare, plus free entertainment. Usually held the last weekend in August.

For more information, contact the Portage Area Chamber of Commerce, (800) 474-2525.

VOYAGE TO THE PORTAGE

Juliette Kinzie.

In 1830, Juliette Magill, a cultured woman living in New England, married John Kinzie, a handsome, intelligent frontiersman who knew 13 Indian dialects. Their wedding trip was a journey to Fort Winnebago, at what is now Portage, where John was to be employed as Indian agent. Juliette recorded her trip (and the succeeding years at the fort and in Chicago) in her diary, which was published in 1856 as *Wau-bun, The "Early Day" in the Northwest.*

Juliette and John, accompanied by Judge James Doty, who later became territorial governor of Wisconsin, were transported in Mackinac boats by French voyageurs. In the following passage Juliette describes her first night and morning in an "encampment" at a site near the present town of Appleton, and gives us a rare view of the pristine wilderness along the Fox River.

The left bank of the river was to the west, and over a portion less elevated than the rest the sun's parting rays fell upon the boat, the men with their red caps and belts, and the two tents already pitched. The smoke now beginning to ascend from the evening fires, the high wooded bank beyond, up which the steep portage path could just be discerned, and, more remote still, the long stretch of waterfall now darkening in the shadow of the overhanging forests, formed a lovely landscape, to which the pencil of an artist could alone do justice.

This was my first encampment, and I was quite enchanted with the novelty of everything about me. ...

The first sound that saluted our ears in the early dawn of the following morning, was the far-reaching call of the bourgeois: "How! how! how!" uttered at the very top of his voice.

The fire is replenished, the kettles set on to boil, the mess-baskets opened, and a portion of their contents brought forth to be made ready for breakfast. One Frenchman spreads our mat within the tent, whence the bedding has all been carefully removed and packed up for stowing in the boat. The tin cups and plates are placed around on the new-fashioned table-cloth. The heavy dews make it a little too damp for us to breakfast in the open air; otherwise our preparations would be made outside, upon the green grass. In an incredibly short time our smoking coffee and boiled ham are placed before us, to which are added, from time to time, slices of toast brought hot and fresh from the glowing coals.

There is, after all, no breakfast like a breakfast in the woods, with a well-trained Frenchman for master of ceremonies.

Everything being at length in readiness, the tents were struck and carried around the Portage, and my husband, the Judge, and I followed at our leisure.

The woods were brilliant with wild flowers, although it was so late in the season the glory of the summer was well-nigh past. But the lupin, the moss-pink, and the yellow wallflower, with all the varieties of the helianthus, the aster, and the solidago, spread their gay charms around. The gentlemen gathered clusters of the bittersweet from the overhanging boughs to make a wreath for my hat, as we trod the tangled pathway.

which Gale resided before her marriage, is now the home of the Women's Civic League, and is open by appointment and for special events.

You'll find downtown Portage to be a genuine working city center, with shoe stores, pharmacies, barber shops and the like rather than tourist-type attractions. If you like antiques, though, be sure to check out the Antiques Mall at 112 W. Cook St., which carries dishes, flatware, a dizzying assembly of wooden chairs, and other odds and ends, all at reasonable prices. Maloney's Antiques, up a squeaky staircase to the second floor of 127½ W. Cook St., has an impressive collection of cut glass and Wedgwood china.

For a snack that can't be beat, stroll down Cook Street to the Market Square parking lot after 8:30 p.m. There, in a small white trailer under a red neon sign, Bob Holch will sell you a bag of fluffy white popcorn (salted, with or without butter) in any of a range of sizes costing from 20 cents to a dollar. He represents the third generation of Holches to pop popcorn for Portage, and a steady stream of customers attests to its flavor and crunch.

IN THE AREA

The countryside to the north and east of Portage seems plucked from a dream: bright green, gently contoured, and wet with marshes and springs that bubble out of the sandy soil. On County F, John Muir Memorial County Park protects a fen containing rare plant species and the land on which Muir, the founder of America's national park system, lived between 1849 and 1855. "Even if I should never see it again," Muir wrote of this place, "the beauty of its lilies and orchids is so pressed into my mind I shall always enjoy looking back at them in my imagination. ..." A boat landing provides access to the lake, and a hiking path leads through a restored prairie. Tables in an oak grove are available for picnicking.

On County CM east of County F, Dates Millpond provides a lovely fishing spot near the old, metal-sided mill. Owner Alice Wilcox charges 50 cents for parking, 50 cents a person to fish from shore and $4 to rent a boat. Leave the money in the tin can near the pond.

Levee Road, a designated Rustic Road just across the Wisconsin River southwest of Portage, winds by the Pine Island State Wildlife Refuge and the site of Aldo Leopold's "Sand County" shack. A tunnel of trees, it's a wonderful route for bicycling; be sure to pause in your pedaling to clamber up on the levee for a look at the languorous river. A drive or bicycle ride down County U to Merrimac will take you past more views of the Wisconsin and, in Merrimac, a working blacksmith shop, ice-cream stands and a free ferry ride.

Farther afield, the Audubon Society's Goose Pond Sanctuary, on Goose Pond Road off Highway 51 south of Portage, harbors flocks of migrating waterfowl in spring and fall. The MacKenzie Environmental Education Center, on County Q/CS south of Portage, contains exhibits of live Wisconsin wildlife, self-guided nature trails (two of which are handicapped accessible) and a logging museum.

The Amish have established a large community northeast of Portage, and the sight of horses and buggies contributes greatly to the area's bucolic personality. On County CM near the Marquette-Green Lake county line, you'll find Mishler's Store, which serves the Amish by stocking such things as stone-ground whole-wheat flour in 50-pound bags, pumpkin butter, ice-cream bases, buckwheat pancake mix, medicinal herbs and homeopathic remedies. The store is open 8 a.m. to 5:30 p.m. every day, except Sunday and Thursday. Some of the area Amish sell furniture from their homes. Look for Schrock's farm, with trellises, gazebos, garden benches and picnic tables made to order on County HH south of Kingston. Please remember that the Amish do not wish to be photographed. ∎

SUMMER
jaunts

Walk scenic trails, bicycle country

roads, canoe down quiet rivers,

explore historic sites, or relax

in a theatre under the stars.

From fragrant pine forests to

pastoral farmfields, Wisconsin's

summer landscape beckons.

PICKS OF THE SEASON

july, august & september

1 HIKING

ON TOP OF OLD PENOKEE

From the ancient Penokee Range juts St. Peter's Dome, a 1,600-foot granite monadnock that forms the highest peak in Chequamegon National Forest. Sturdy shoes, and a lot of heavy breathing, will take you to the summit, where you'll find one of the most expansive wilderness views in the state. The two-mile trail starts from Forest Road 199, which runs along the border of Bayfield and Ashland counties south of County E. Call (715) 762-2461 for more information.

Turtle-Flambeau Scenic Waters Area.

2 EVENT

LUMBERJACK WORLD CHAMPIONSHIPS

A really good lumberjack, it was said, could throw a bar of soap into the water and ride the bubbles to shore. With the logging era long past, we have little opportunity to observe such feats, except, that is, at the Lumberjack World Championships held in Hayward the last full weekend in July. Loggers have assembled here since 1959. Axes ring, sawdust flies, and legs scramble as contestants chop wood, dash up incredibly tall poles, and madly spin floating logs. It is a colorful—and hugely entertaining—reminder of the mighty men who felled Wisconsin's vast forests. For exact dates, call (715) 634-2484.

3 CANOEING

PADDLING PARADISE

In 1990, the state purchased nearly the entire Turtle-Flambeau Flowage—23,576 acres, the largest land purchase in Wisconsin's history. The plan is to keep it as it is, because "as it is" is exquisite.

Besides nearly 14,000 acres of water, the protected area includes 145 islands and 12,000 acres of surrounding woods and wetlands, all of it wild and unsettled. Eagles, ospreys and loons are found here in greater abundance than anywhere else

Log-rolling at the Lumberjack World Championships.

in Wisconsin.

If you canoe, you'll find few places better than what is now called the Turtle-Flambeau Scenic Waters Area. For a brochure containing information on fishing, camping and boating regulations, call the DNR ranger station in Mercer at (715) 476-2240.

4 ARTS

FOLK ART WONDER AT CONCRETE PARK

At Fred Smith's Concrete Park in Price County, angels and Indians, mythical characters and old friends stand eternally posed, crafted of concrete, chicken wire, shards of broken mirrors and beer bottles. For years the work was considered a curiosity—even weird. The Kohler Foundation purchased the park, with its 203 figures, and restored it as a masterpiece of folk art. It sits on Highway 13 south of Phillips, a testament to the splendor of one man's unfettered vision. Call (715) 339-6371 for more information.

5 NATURE

SEEING STARS

If you'd like to see the moon and stars appearing 200 times larger and 10,000 times brighter, visit the Hobbs Observatory in Beaver Creek Reserve. You'll be able to view the skies up close through telescopes every clear Saturday night May through October (and every clear third Saturday of the month between November and April). In addition, the center offers a program, usually with a speaker, every third Saturday of the month at 8 p.m., year-round, when skies are clear. The Wise Nature Center is nearby, containing a discovery room with hands-on learning stations. Or just hike around. Self-guided interpretive trails wind throughout the 360-acre reserve, north of Fall Creek on County K. Call (715) 877-2212 for hours.

6 NATURE

ROAMING THE NICOLET

The Nicolet National Forest was established by presi-

Two of the 203 figures at Fred Smith's Concrete Park.

dential proclamation in 1933, but the land, its wildlife and its people were already here. Paleo-Indians inhabited the region 10,000 years ago. Generations of Native Americans camped here, fur traders passed through, and, at the turn of the century, lumbermen left their mark—felling most of the great forest. When the cutover proved unsuitable for farming, the federal government bought the land and planted thousands of acres of pine trees. Today the new forest provides habitat once again for fish and wildlife, along with a multitude of recreational opportunies.

In the summer, the forest is easily explored on foot. Numerous trails wind around the woods, lakes and streams. Among the most scenic: the Anvil Trail loop complex and Franklin Lake Trail, a one-mile interpretive trail leading through a tamarack swamp and relic stands of hemlocks and towering white pines. The Anvil Lake Trail is eight and a half miles east of Eagle River on Highway 70. To get to the Franklin Lake Trail, take Highway 70 nine miles east of Eagle River to Forest Road 2178, drive south three miles to Forest Road 2181, and then drive east five miles to the Franklin Lake campground. For more information, call the Nicolet National Forest Laona Ranger District at (715) 674-4481.

7 EVENT

WHITEWATER!

Most whitewater kayaking takes place on furious wilderness rivers, making it hard to observe this thrilling

Running the course at Wausau's Whitewater Park.

sport unless you want to actually be in the boat yourself. An exception is in Wausau. Here at Whitewater Park, a premier canoe and kayak course cuts through the center of the city on what was the east channel of the Wisconsin River. International championship races are hosted each summer, giving spectators a unique opportunity to view world-class paddlers battle the big waves. For dates, contact the Wausau Area Convention and Visitors Council, (800) 236-WSAU.

Fun at the Fox Cities Children's Museum.

Door County's Peninsula Players.

36

8 MUSEUM

FOR THE KIDS

"Whatever you do, plan to stay a minimum of two hours." That's the friendly advice of the executive director of the Fox Cities Children's Museum in Appleton to parents and grandparents planning a first visit to Wisconsin's largest children's museum. When you consider that the museum boasts 16 hands-on exhibit areas covering 27,000 square feet, the advice is well worth heeding or it will be a long car ride home with the little ones.

Located in the Avenue Mall in downtown Appleton, the museum is designed for ages 2 to 12, but the lively, colorful atmosphere will appeal to children of all ages. Here's just a sampling of the exhibits: "Trains, Planes, Boats & More," where children can take the controls of everything from a sailboat to a flight simulator; "Kids' Care Clinic," with its doctor's office and crawl-through heart chambers; and "Creation Station," where local paper products and other recyclables can be transformed into works of art and later displayed—where else?—on a wall of brightly painted refrigerator doors. Museum hours are 9 a.m. to 5 p.m. Monday through Thursday; 9 a.m. to 8 p.m. Friday; 10 a.m. to 5 p.m. Saturday; and noon to 5 p.m.

Sunday. Children under 17 are not admitted without an adult. Call (414) 734-3226 for more information.

9 ARTS

THEATRE UNDER THE STARS

Door County's Peninsula Players is the oldest continuously operating theater of its kind in the United States, "its kind" being resident theater, in which the actors and actresses live in dormitories on the grounds, take their meals together, and coexist in an atmosphere of creative synergy. But that's not all that distinguishes Peninsula Players from most other theater companies. The setting, under the stars at the water's edge near Fish Creek, is magical. And the actors, with credits that extend from Broadway to Hollywood and beyond, exude the sheer, undiluted joy of their craft. Both classic and contemporary dramas and comedies are performed during a summer season that runs from late June through mid-October. For tickets, call (414) 868-3287.

10 BICYCLING

RIDING THE RAILS

In 1870, the Chicago North Western line passed through one of the most picturesque portions of Wisconsin on its route from Madison to Sparta.

But it came at tremendous expense. The landscape here was dense with steep-sided hills, from which numerous springs sent shafts of clear, cold water that threatened to erode the track. Three tunnels had to be gouged, one of which—three-quarters of a mile long—took three years to build, all with hand tools, horses and oxen.

After highways replaced railroads, the line was abandoned. But rather than waste all this hard labor, the state, in 1965, purchased 32 miles of the Chicago and North Western's main line. From it was created the nation's first railroad-grade bicycling trail. Today, the Elroy-Sparta Trail is our most popular bicycling route, with beautiful vistas, historic displays and three long, dark tunnels filled with railroading ghosts.

For more information, call the trail headquarters in Kendall at (608) 463-7109.

11 DRIVING TOUR

FARM VISITS

How often have you driven down a country lane, spied a picturesque farm, and wanted to pull in? The urge seems especially strong in southwest Wisconsin, where fields and pastures stretch over ridges, and farmhouses tuck into valleys to form an unspoiled, pastoral landscape.

Wright-designed Romeo and Juliet windmill.

Feel frustrated no more. A brochure, "Farm Trails Thru Scenic Southwest Wisconsin," will lead you to more than two dozen farms and rural businesses in the region whose owners invite everybody to come and visit. Many farms in this area grow organic produce. Some turn out less typical products, such as wool yarns, unpasteurized honey and gourmet popcorn. Others are traditional dairy farms.

Each farm sets its own hours for visiting; the Farm Trails brochure provides details and a map. For a copy, send a self-addressed business-size envelope to Farm Trails, 4478 Riley Rd., Boscobel, WI 53805.

12 ARTS

WRIGHT ON!

Thanks to a special Taliesin tour, fans of Frank Lloyd Wright can take a comprehensive look at the buildings and land that continue to function in a manner faithful to Wright's vision. "These buildings are rare in that they are still living," says Taliesin's manager. "Architecture is still learned and created here, beans and corn are planted on a working farm—it's just as Wright envisioned."

Tour-goers will see architects and apprentices at work in the Hillside Studio, stroll through gardens and courtyards, and traverse the softly rolling hills that inspired Wright to build here. Models and current architectural projects are displayed.

Taliesin, which is located on Highway 23 south of Spring Green, is open for tours May through October. Call (608) 588-7900 for details and making reservations.

13 EVENT
A HISTORIC FOURTH

In the midst of a lazy day off, it's easy to forget that the Fourth of July is a patriotic occasion. But not at Stonefield Village. Here the State Historical Society celebrates America's independence just as Wisconsinites did in the 1890s in small towns throughout the state.

An old-fashioned parade is followed by an oration, music and games for the children. Visitors will want to tour the entire historic site, which includes a charming re-created turn-of-the-century village and the state agricultural museum. Stonefield is located one mile north of Cassville on County VV in Grant County. Call (608) 725-5210 for hours.

14 CANOEING
LAZY DOWN THE WISCONSIN RIVER

You may have already paddled the Wisconsin between Sauk City and Spring Green, one of the most popular canoe routes in the state.

Less well-traveled and far wilder in spirit is the stretch from Blue River to the confluence with the Mississippi. Hauling your canoe through ankle-deep water, drifting for long stretches between high bluffs and low scrub devoid of any sign of settlement, you feel almost lost in time. For a truly transporting experience, camp overnight on a sandbar, and let your soul open to the darkness and the dazzling expanse of stars overhead. Call (608) 375-2672 for information on canoe rentals.

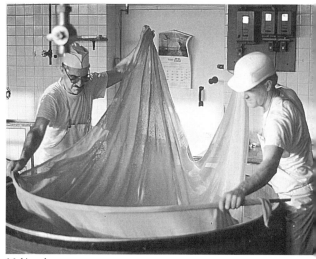

Making cheese.

15 SHOPPING
CHALET CHEESE

When it comes to separating the curds from the whey, no one does it better than Wisconsin cheesemakers. And they do it all: Muenster, Swiss, gouda, provolone, string, gorgonzola, Parmesan, brick, Colby (the latter two developed in Wisconsin) and Limburger, that most aromatic of cheeses. Limburger cheese-making, however, is a specialty. In fact, Chalet Cheese Co-op in Monroe, founded in 1885, is today the only manufacturer in the country producing Limburger cheese. Stop by the factory on County N north of Monroe for a taste. Call (608) 325-4343 for hours.

Pitching shocks at the Dodge County Antique Power Show.

16 EVENT

OLD-TIME THRESHEREE

A sharp whistle slices the air. Dusky, sooty smoke puffs from coal-fired engines. Men in denim overalls pitch bundles of oats into the mouths of waiting machines. Various contraptions growl, clunk, cough, wheeze and purr. Altogether, the noise is clam-orous, the action terribly exciting—just as it was on "thrashin' day" a hundred years ago. The date, though, is the first full weekend in August, and the event is the Dodge County Antique Power Club's Antique Power, Steam and Threshing Show.

On the club's showgrounds at the intersection of county highways B and I near Burnett, collectors from throughout the country work in crews to display not only threshing machines but corn harvesting machinery, antique hay balers, a working sawmill and other smaller implements. These are powered by mammoth coal-burning steam engines, early farm tractors and primitive flywheel gas engines. Other activities usually scheduled include an antique tractor parade, tractor pull, flea market and corn roast. Call (414) 386-2441 for details.

17 SHOPPING

ANTIQUES MECCA

It's the same from Bayfield to Sturgeon Bay: The best inns all feature fabulous antiques. And when you ask the owners where they snared such terrific pieces, one town keeps popping up—Princeton. Although Princeton, in Green Lake County, dubs itself "The Antiques Center of Mid-Wisconsin," it would be nearer the truth to call it the antiques

center of the entire state.
In addition to fine shops,
there's an antiques mall and,
on Saturdays through mid-
October, a wonderful flea
market. Call (414) 295-3877
for more information.

18 MUSEUM

WISCONSIN MARITIME MUSEUM OF HISTORY

W hat child—or adult,
for that matter—could
resist a museum that features a
genuine World War II subma-
rine? Exploring the USS Cobia,
now berthed in the Manitowoc
River, is a fascinating lesson in
how sailors lived and worked
deep below the ocean waves a
half-century ago. Inside the
adjacent museum building,
photographs and exhibits explain 100 years of Great Lakes
maritime history. The museum,
located at 75 Maritime Drive in
Manitowoc, is open daily. Call
(414) 684-0218.

19 MUSEUM

A SHRINE FOR THE DAIRY INDUSTRY

W ho, more than any
other individual, can
be credited with bringing
dairy to the Dairy State? Most
historians will tell you it was
former Gov. William D. Hoard,
a native New York Stater who
in the mid-1800s promoted
dairying as the road to agricul-

*Exploring the Wisconsin Maritime Museum of History.
Below: Butter churn at the Dairy Shrine.*

tural survival for Wisconsin
wheat farmers troubled by
dwindling yields.

So began the industry that's
shaped and defined our state
more than any other, and the
Dairy Shrine in Fort Atkinson
is the place to go if you'd like
to learn more about it. Scores
of artifacts are here—a
dog-powered tread-
mill once hooked to a
butter churn, for
example—to remind
visitors just how far
dairying has come in
its 8,000-year history.
Curious minds can
take in an 18-minute
audio-visual show
that covers every-
thing from animal
nutrition to artificial

41

insemination, check out the blanket worn at the 1939 World's Fair by Elsie the Cow (of Borden fame), or glimpse dairying's future in a "tomorrow" exhibit.

Proving that pumping out 60 pounds of milk every day is in no way a thankless job, the Shrine displays photos honoring breed-show grand champions, diagrams explaining the differences among the six dairy breeds and numerous other exhibits celebrating cows.

The Dairy Shrine is connected to the Hoard Historical Museum, a museum of local history, on Highway 12 in Fort Atkinson. For hours, call (414) 563-7769.

20 MUSEUM

OLD WORLD WISCONSIN

Spread across 576 acres in the Kettle Moraine State Forest near Eagle, Old World Wisconsin includes more than 50 historic structures gathered from all corners of the state. But this is not just a collection of aging buildings. Here the State Historical Society preserves structures that especially reflect the architectural traditions of our state's ethnic settlers. Wander its grounds and you'll find, for example, a Norwegian log cabin, a seven-building turn-of-the-century Finnish farm and a thatch-covered barn built in a half-timbered pattern brought to America by German immigrants. Each homestead has been painstakingly restored and each is inhabited by costumed interpreters who cook, spin, work the fields, and recount for visitors the story of each building and its original owners.

Old World Wisconsin is located south of Eagle on Highway 67 and is open daily from May through October. For more information, call (414) 594-2116.

Threshing time at Old World Wisconsin.

weekend ADVENTURES

Delight in
Stockholm,
a quaint
river town;
explore the
stunning
Apostle Islands;
and sample
the grandeur
of Lake Geneva,
one of Wisconsin's
oldest resort
communities.

BAYFIELD

STOCKHOLM

LAKE GENEVA

BAYFIELD

Lake Superior's Beautiful Bayfield

Bayfield is the gateway to a sprawling freshwater archipelago, the Apostle Islands, whose austere and rigorous beauty cuts to the deepest chambers of the heart. But the crux of Bayfield's attraction is the way the built environment of the village, perched on a hillside like a magical gingerbread fiefdom, balances so precisely with the natural one. The people, too, are part of this, a quirky and eclectic mix of natives and transplants whose collective ambitions have maintained a

Bayfield Harbor.

properly human scale. The upshot is that in few places can one feel such a complete sense of well-being, of karmic serenity.

There is a comfortable antiquity, as well. The Ojibway have lived here for centuries. Pierre Le Sueur established a fur-trading post on the largest Apostle, Madeline Island, in 1693. Entrepreneur Henry Rice platted Bayfield in 1857. Fortunes were made in logging (for a time so many lumber mills operated in the area that the water was covered with a film of sawdust) and in the quarrying of native brownstone. In the 19th century, the rich shoals of the Apostles yielded enormous catches of whitefish, lake trout and herring, which were shipped all over the country. But only such commerce as could be sustained survived: fishing, limited farming and tourism. Seeking to escape summer heat, vacationers discovered Bayfield over a century ago, and have never stopped coming.

It's easy to understand why. You'll find some of the best visits here are lazy ones. Stroll through the sacred Ojibway burial grounds on Madeline Island, and look for the dates on the weathered stones. Then, traveling from the sublime to the ridiculous, drink beers in the shade of the palm fronds at Tom's Burnt-Down Cafe. Order sandwiches to go from the Beach Club in

La Pointe, then trek to Big Bay State Park, where the water is not only inviting but actually tolerable (a rare occurrence for this frigid Lake Superior). Most of all, enjoy a lovely, languorous interlude in a

Village of Bayfield, perched on a hillside.

beautiful setting, the sun bright, the sand warm, the water sparkling.

The point is, Wisconsin's northern tip is the kind of place where you can do essentially nothing and still feel utterly fulfilled. Herewith then, a guide to whatever tickles your fancy—or doesn't—in and around Bayfield and the Apostles.

Beach at Sand Island.

AREA HISTORY

A required first stop for anyone new to the area is the National Park Service Visitor's Center, located in the massive native brownstone building in Bayfield that was once the county courthouse. The exhibits detail the region's history—geological, biological and human—and chronicle the ups and downs of its commercial enterprises. Every Wednesday evening during the summer, the Around the Archipelago Guest Lecture Series addresses topics of particular relevance.

The commercial fishing heritage of Lake Superior is on display at the Hokenson Brothers Fishery at Little Sand Bay north of Bayfield, on the cusp of the peninsula; Park Service personnel conduct interpretive tours throughout the summer. On Stockton Island, naturalists acquaint visitors with the flora and fauna that have adapted to what is basically a subarctic climate. The Madeline Island Historical Museum, housed in what was once the American Fur Company headquarters, emphasizes the sometimes hostile, sometimes cordial interactions between Native Americans and French fur traders and missionaries.

The premier cultural entertainment in the area is the Big Top Chautauqua. In a

EATING WELL

Old Rittenhouse Inn—Dinner here is not merely a meal but an event. The menu is related verbally in mouth-watering detail; regional, seasonal specialties— fresh lake trout, locally raised lamb, flavorful wild mushrooms— are featured whenever possible, and desserts are spectacular. Reservations required. 301 Rittenhouse Ave. (715) 779-5111.

The Clubhouse on Madeline Island—Insiders say this restaurant is Rittenhouse's equal when it comes to elegant, imaginative cuisine. Sophisticated food, served in a modern, spacious dining room with a view of the golf course and lake, is complemented by the finest wine list north of Madison. Open May to October with free shuttle service from the island ferry. (715) 747-2612.

Maggie's—The flamingos are fake but the food is real, with hearty, homemade soups, an astonishing variety of burgers, luscious desserts and the best sauteed whitefish livers in town. 257 Manypenny. (715) 779-5641.

Greunke's First Street Inn— With tongue planted firmly in cheek, Greunke's embodies the nostalgic, neon ambiance of a 1940s diner. This is where the wise gather for breakfast, especially when the raspberries are in season and adorn a stack of light-as-air pancakes, topped with a Matterhorn of whipped cream. 17 N. First St. (715) 779-5480.

LODGING

Old Rittenhouse Inn—The inn's 20 guest rooms, all with fireplaces and private baths, are located in three historic homes. This is the last word in pampered luxury. (715) 779-5111.

Pinehurst Inn—A cozy B&B with country charm. (715) 779-3676.

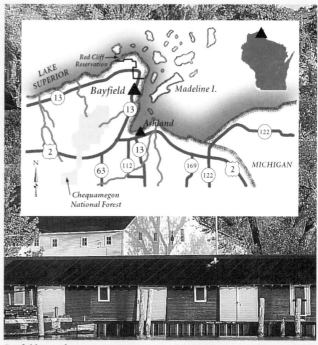

Bayfield waterfront.

Cooper Hill House—Comfortable lodging, with private baths, in an 1888 home. (715) 779-5060.

Seagull Bay Motel—Clean rooms, low rates and a splendid view of Lake Superior. (715) 779-5558.

Camping—Available at Big Bay State Park (a state park sticker is required) and Big Bay Town Park on Madeline Island; both parks charge a fee. You can also camp on most of the other islands that make up the Apostle Islands National Lakeshore. Pick up a free permit at the National Park Service Visitor's Center.

SUMMER EVENTS

Inland Sea Symposium— Evening programs on the fragile Lake Superior ecosystem complement workshops on every aspect of the sport of kayaking. Held in June.

Red Cliff Powwow—Honors Ojibway chief Henry Buffalo with drumming and dancing. Held during Fourth of July weekend.

Bayfield Race Week—A colorful, open-to-all regatta features the 60-mile Around the Islands race and numerous shorter contests. Held the last week of June.

Wooden Boat and Maritime Heritage Festival—Traditional wooden vessels of all descriptions sail to Bayfield Harbor. Held in August.

IN OTHER SEASONS

Bayfield Apple Festival— Foodstands galore, street entertainers, apple-peeling and pie-baking contests, capped off by a festival parade. Buy apples at a local orchard to take home. Held the first weekend in October. *For more information, contact the Bayfield Chamber of Commerce at (715) 779-3335.*

ANANDA

Many experienced sailors are of the opinion that the Apostle Islands offer the finest freshwater sailing in North America—if not the world. And of all the vessels that ply these impossibly beautiful waters, there is perhaps none so lovely as Ananda, a 56-foot wooden schooner. With her classic lines, distinctive gaff-rigged foresail and gleaming brightwork, she conjures up the romance of a bygone era. In point of fact, though, Ananda was christened only in 1994, a year and a half after she began to take shape in Mike Caswell's Bayfield boat shop. Another remarkable thing about Ananda: You can charter her.

Schooner Ananda.

A boat-builder since the early 1980s, Caswell decided in 1991 that he wanted to captain his own Lake Superior charter sailboat. His first inclination was to purchase an older vessel in reasonably good condition and repair and restore it as necessary. When that option proved impractical, he did the next best thing: He bought a 1929 Alden schooner that was OK but not quite worth overhauling, salvaged everything he could, and began building a new boat to put the old parts on. Although Caswell did use some contemporary construction techniques, Ananda is in all other respects a traditional wooden schooner. Granted, her name is a little unusual. It's Sanscrit for "the joy without which the universe would collapse."

In addition to Caswell and crew, Ananda can carry up to six passengers. You can charter her for a half-day, a day, a weekend or a week, and if you ask nicely the captain might even let you take the helm for a reach or two.

For more information, write or call Caswell's Boat Shop, P.O. Box 182, Bayfield, WI 54814; (800) 300-7770 or (715) 779-5774.

striped circus tent on Mount Ashwabay, this Chautauqua inspires, educates, and entertains, as did the chautauquas of the 19th century after which it is patterned. Offerings range from lectures on photography to ethnic song and dance to musical revues based on Bayfield Peninsula history. Listening, watching, and enjoying, as a summer breeze wafts over you and ripples the giant canvas, is one of this region's most delightful experiences.

As for arts and crafts, there must be more artists—especially potters—on the Bayfield Peninsula than anywhere else in the state. Be sure to check out Eckels Pottery Shop, which contains everything you can imagine made of stoneware and porcelain, on the south edge of Bayfield, and Karlyn's Gallery, which features the work of a number of area artists, in nearby Washburn.

RECREATION

With their deep, protected harbors, wild shorelines and prevailing winds, Bayfield and the Apostles have long been a mecca for sailors. Sailboats Inc. and Superior Charters, among others, offer captained and bareboat charters, customized to a client's specifications. Guided sea kayak trips and paddling instruction can be arranged through Trek and Trail. (Sign up for the trip to the Squaw Bay sea caves, which verges on a religious experience.) A number of trolling ships ply the depths for trout and salmon; one of the best is Roberta's Sport Fishing Charter.

If you have neither your own boat nor a rented one, you can travel to Madeline Island on the Madeline Island Ferry Line. Regularly scheduled shuttles operated by the Apostle Islands Cruise Service will take you to the other islands. You can also arrange to be dropped off and picked up by one of their water taxis. The company also offers tours. For a glimpse of the area's richly textured past, sign on for the one that stops at historic Raspberry Island Lighthouse and the funky Manitou Island Fish Camp.

On terra firma, the Madeline Island Golf Club, with its unique, double-greened Robert Trent Jones layout, is a treat for both the confirmed duffer and the low-handicapper. On the mainland, the relatively new Apostle Highlands course is still a few years from maturity, but has a dazzling view of Lake Superior.

And don't miss Bayfield's best recreational event: At sunrise, golden light pours into this east-facing village like water into a cup. It's the best vantage point in the state—fill your thermos with high-octane coffee some night, and set the alarm for dawn. ■

STOCKHOLM

Stockholm, A Tiny Town on the Great River Road

The Great River Road snakes up the western border of Wisconsin, caught between the Mississippi River and huge, craggy bluffs until it reaches Lake Pepin. In this rumpled, rugged countryside, broad Lake Pepin—three miles wide and 30 miles long—is a welcome surprise. In the 19th century, immigrants flocked to it, including large numbers of Swedes, who founded a town halfway up the Wisconsin shoreline, which they ambitiously named Stockholm. Here, settlers thrived, selling grain, fish, cordwood and ice from the big lake. The 20th century brought change, however: first, a decline, as river traffic snubbed the little town in favor of bigger cities, and then, happily, prosperity. Today, Stockholm is a tourist destination, with renovated storefronts, tempting shops, fine restaurants and a glorious setting that never goes out of style.

Quilts and furniture at Amish Country.

THE VILLAGE

Stockholm is centered around the intersection of Highway 35 and Spring Street, a mere handful of Victorian homes and historic buildings. At night the streets are empty, the only signs of life coming from trains thundering through and the flickering lights from campfires in the Village Park. Lake Pepin lies one block to the west; steep bluffs rise to the sky two blocks east. B&B owner Lee Krebs laughs when he says, "I always tell guests there is absolutely nothing to do here." But Krebs knows, and visitors quickly discover, the charm of Stockholm lies in that serenity.

By day, however, Stockholm transforms. In the lower level of a Victorian house on Spring Street, Ruth Raich rises early to bake the breads and pastries for which her Jenny Lind Cafe is famous. By 9 a.m. the coffee is perked, the tables in the adjoining garden dusted off, and a line has formed of customers who can't decide between a rich caramel roll or the muffin of the day. Conversations indicate some of the clientele is local but most are visitors cognizant of Stockholm's stock-in-trade: shopping. A dozen gift stores, art galleries and antiques shops line Stockholm's main streets. The largest building in town, on the corner of Spring Street and Highway 35, belongs to Amish Country,

which specializes in quilts and baskets handmade by Wisconsin Amish women, and furniture by Indiana Amish. There is plenty of room here to hang quilts on the walls and set up four-poster beds—originally a general store, the building was made large enough to include an opera house on the second level, complete with stage. Those hunting for historic treasures browse through the collectibles at Stockholm Antiques. Formerly the town's harness factory, the shop is as old as some of the pieces on display. Across the street, River Road Antiques features fine Early American furniture, primitives and silver. Next door, Crocus Oak Co. and Hickory Hollow offer in-the-rough antique furniture.

Fanciful iron sculptures by Ellis Nelson stand in the small yard outside the Red Balloon Gallery, a wonderful showcase for regional art. Inside, more than 70 artists, working in a variety of media, are represented, along with a collection of patterned African baskets. Exquisite, hand-painted silk garments are the centerpiece of Spirit of the River. The unusual earrings at B and B Exotics, made from carp and garfish scales, shine like mica.

Shopping done, you'll want to head for the Village Park to picnic under the trees, lounge on a sand beach, and dabble in Lake Pepin's clear water. Stop

STOCKHOLM'S SWEDES

Shortly before 1850 (historians don't know the exact date), Erik Petersson, a young man from Varmland, Sweden, left his homeland to seek his fortune in the goldfields of California. He never reached the West, however, working instead as a lumberjack and raftsman on the St. Croix River. When exploring the country near Lake Pepin in 1851, he made the decision to found a settlement there. A brother, Anders, arrived in 1853 with a party of immigrants, and the following year Erik brought over 200 Swedes from Varmland to America. Though more than half died of cholera on the journey, many of the survivors continued with Erik to the shores of Lake Pepin, where they named their new town Stockholm. It was the first Swedish settlement in western Wisconsin.

Swedish immigrant family, 1896.

by the post office, too, to view old photographs and letters written in Swedish that recall Stockholm's early days. Evening, of course, is the time for strolling, as sleepy Stockholm tucks itself in for the night awash in cool, lake-scented air.

IN THE AREA

Rustic Road 51, which departs from County AA a few miles north of town, takes you into coulee country, a land of narrow valleys and sandstone ridges. The winding gravel road pierces a dense woods, picturesquely crossing and recrossing a trout stream before it opens onto ridgetop farmfields.

From there, take the back roads or return to Highway 35 to reach Stockholm's neighboring villages. Maiden Rock to the north, and Pepin, Nelson and Alma to the south all contain their share of galleries, shops and cafes. Maiden Rock, set in Lake Pepin's bend, also features a fantastic 25-mile-long view. Outside of Pepin on County CC rests a replica of the Little House in the Big Woods, Laura Ingalls Wilder's birthplace. Alma is an architecture buff's joy: The entire town is listed on the National Register of Historic Places. Nelson marks the northern gateway to the Upper Mississippi River National Wildlife and Fish Refuge, 200,000 acres of wooded islands, river channels and marshes that extend to Rock Island, Ill. The refuge harbors 292 species of birds, 50 species of mammals and 118 species of fish. Drive the Great River Road south of Nelson in the spring, and you'll see bald eagles feeding in the river. Thousands of tundra swans stop in the area between early October and mid-November. Three miles north of Alma, at Reick's Park, an observation platform is staffed during peak viewing times. Sportsmen fish the refuge year-round for walleye, bass, perch, crappies, sunfish and catfish. Primitive camping is allowed on refuge beaches for up to 14 days. ∎

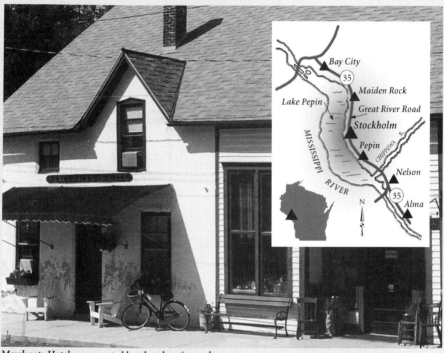

Merchants Hotel, a renovated hotel and antiques shop.

EATING WELL

Jenny Lind Cafe & Bakery—Fresh-baked breads and pastries send out tantalizing aromas from a Victorian house in Stockholm. Have a cardamom roll for breakfast, homemade sandwich and soup for lunch, and take home a loaf of Swedish limpa bread. Open mid-March to late-December. 114 Spring St. (715) 442-2358.

Harbor View Cafe—Gourmet selections change daily; grilled salmon and Kahlua cheesecake are sure bets when available. Reservations are not accepted here so arrive early. Open March through mid-November. First and Main streets in Pepin. (715) 442-3893.

Beth's Twin Bluffs Cafe—Country cooking fills you up at this family restaurant in Nelson. Be sure to leave room for a slice of fresh-baked pie. Located on Highway 35. (715) 673-4040.

Pier 4 Cafe—It's hard to beat the $1.99 breakfast or catfish special. The cafe's small quarters expand in summer to a screened-in porch overlooking Lock and Dam #4. Highway 35, Alma. (608) 685-4964.

LODGING

Merchants Hotel—Stockholm's renovated historic hotel still caters to overnight visitors with three charming bedrooms and a spacious front porch. (715) 442-2113 or (715) 448-2508.

Great River B&B—This stucco-covered stone home is the oldest in Stockholm, built in 1869. (800) 657-4756.

Hyggelig Hus B&B—This B&B, located in Stockholm, reflects the area's heritage with Scandinavian decor, cooking and hospitality. (715) 442-2086.

Pine Creek Lodge B&B—In the woods about 5 miles north of Stockholm, this new post and beam home surrounds guests with the atmosphere of a country lodge. (715) 448-3203.

SUMMER EVENTS

Art Fair in the Park—Regional artists flock to Stockholm on the third Saturday in July to display their wares under colorful canopies in the Village Park. Food offerings tempt all palates, and musicians play all day. Special Art Fair in the Park posters are available for sale—an original piece is produced by a different artist each year.

IN OTHER SEASONS

Country Christmas—Caroling, hay rides and a visit from Santa Claus himself. Held the first weekend in December.

For more information, contact Amish Country, Box 36, Stockholm, WI 54769; (715) 442-2015.

LAKE GENEVA

The Grandeur of Lake Geneva

At the turn of the century, when Chicago was flexing its industrial muscle, Lake Geneva was the summer home of the rich and powerful. The setting was gorgeous: a clear-blue, spring-fed glacial lake (Geneva Lake), seven miles long and two miles wide at its broadest point.

The area had begun developing as a tourist destination in the 1860s, after the Chicago North Western Railroad extended a line from Chicago, just 75 miles away,

Strolling the Shore Path.

to the town. By 1879 as many as 10 trains a day were pulling into Geneva Station, including a weekend service known as the "Millionaire's Special." By 1910, all the lakeshore property, with the exception of a few public beaches, was transformed into private resorts and estates.

The summer "homes" were, in reality, palaces. Multistoried, with generous porches, turrets and elaborate stonework, surrounded by lush gardens and carefully landscaped lawns, they rimmed Geneva Lake like a necklace of jewels. Their owners—which included such magnates as Wrigley, Swift, Maytag, Crane and Drake—named them fancifully: Maple Lawn, Fair Field, Gay Lynne, Bonnie Brae, Folly, Tyrawley, Loramoor. One owner, R. R. Chandler, bought a reproduction of a Buddhist temple that had been the Ceylon government's exhibit at the 1893 Columbian Exposition, transported it to Lake Geneva, and moved in—after building an elaborate addition and constructing a feudal-style tunnel that connected its basement to the water's edge.

Each year, privileged Victorians spent "the season" here. Old photographs depict quite a vision: thoroughbred horses in the paddocks, tea parties in the gazebos, parasoled ladies strolling the paths, and steam-driven yachts cruising the pel-

A wealth of shops in downtown Lake Geneva.

lucid lake. A century later, visitors' activities are somewhat different. But Lake Geneva remains a grand resort destination, and it still casts a midsummer spell.

THE LAKE AND THE TOWN

As ever, the lake is the center of attention. For an introduction, take yourself down to the Riviera Concourse, an elegant 1932 structure in which Tommy Dorsey and Louis Armstrong once played. Today, the Lake Geneva Cruise Line boat tours depart from the docks. All tours glide by the fancy mansions and include entertaining and informative commentary on Lake Geneva history and lore. One- and two-hour tours are offered, along with lunch, brunch, dinner and ice-cream-social cruises. A two-and-a-half hour trip on the U.S. Mailboat Walworth II includes a special treat: watching agile mail carriers leap from the boat to dockside mailboxes and back to the boat—which never stops moving. Call (800) 558-5911 or (414) 248-6206 for reservations.

You can also rent your own sailboat, speedboat, pontoon boat, ski boat, fishing boat, paddle boat or waverunner at Marina Bay Boat Rentals (414-248-4477), Gordy's (414-275-2163) or Jerry's (414-275-5222). The Wisconsin Sailing School (414-245-5531) offers private sailing lessons and weekend and five-day courses.

One of the most pleasant ways to take in the scenery is on foot. Town law requires that landowners maintain 3 feet of public access around Geneva Lake's perimeter. The 26-mile Shore Path, which traverses the lawns of all the elegant places, gives you a unique, close-up view of gleaming piers, elegant boathouses, manicured gar-

dens, ornate chimneys and elaborate porches. As for logistics, the appropriately named *Walk, Talk & Gawk*, available for purchase in local stores, provides maps and information on points of interest. Pick a segment, start at a given point, walk a ways, and come back. Or, if you don't want to backtrack, arrange for a Lake Geneva tour boat to pick you up at Williams Bay. Contact the ticket office for reservations.

To experience the plush life yourself, check into one of the area's resorts, like the 355-room Grand Geneva Resort & Spa. Built for Hugh Hefner in 1968 as the Playboy Resort & Golf Club, the complex has recently undergone a $20 million refurbishing by the Marcus Corporation. It sits on 1,300 secluded acres and comes with a private lake, ski hill, riding stables, two championship golf courses, indoor and outdoor pools, tennis courts and other exercise facilities. Plus, there's a full-fledged spa for melting away all the worries of everyday life.

The town itself sports some nifty stores, housed in historic buildings on Main and Broad streets. Uncle Gumby's Lakewear features the kind of casual-but-elegant garments that are so perfect for resort settings. Handknit Aran sweaters, for sale at Flemings Ltd., would ward off any

EATING WELL

Popeye's Galley & Grog—A boisterous Lake Geneva institution since 1959, Popeye's features Bionic Burgers on marble rye, homestyle dinners and Greek specialties. 811 Wrigley Dr. (414) 248-4381.

The Open Window—This small cafe, operated by Botticelli's of Madison, serves baguette sandwiches and fine pastries, along with specialty coffees and teas. 724 Main St. (414) 249-1911.

The Grandview Restaurant & Lounge—Elegant American fare in the Geneva Inn's lakeside dining room includes Atlantic salmon, swordfish and veal. N2009 Highway 120. (414) 248-5690.

Fred's Wagon Wheel—Off the beaten path in Delavan but well worth the trip, Fred's specializes in German entrees, lake perch and soft-shell crab. 3103 County O. (414) 728-8831.

The Cheese Box—The oldest cheese store in the area will rent you an insulated backpack and stock it with sandwiches and picnic paraphernalia—perfect for a lakeshore stroll. 801 Wells St. (800) 345-6105.

French Quarter Beignets—This tiny outlet in the Riviera Concourse will also pack you lunch to go (24-hours' notice required). Make sure you sample the renowned New Orleans doughnuts. (414) 249-0599.

LODGING

Grand Geneva Resort & Spa—A full-service resort with every amenity you can think of, including a luxurious spa. (800) 558-3417.

The Geneva Inn—This English country inn-style getaway is located right on Lake Geneva. Bring your boat and tie it up at the dock. (414) 248-5680.

Roses—Three blocks from downtown, this very comfortable bed and breakfast inn welcomes guests

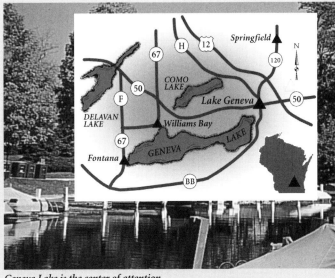

Geneva Lake is the center of attention.

with afternoon tea and sherry. (414) 248-4344.

Pederson Victorian Bed & Breakfast—A magnificent Victorian home three miles north of Lake Geneva in Springfield, Pederson forgoes TVs, telephones and whirlpools for a serene setting, vegetarian breakfasts and an environment-friendly policy that assures all linens have been line-dried. (414) 248-9110.

Lake Geneva Campus of George Williams College—The conference center offers housekeeping cottages that are somewhat worn but a bargain for families. The lakeside setting is beautiful, and nature trails, a golf course, and volleyball and badminton courts are right there on campus. (414) 245-5531.

Big Foot Beach State Park—Named after a Potawatomi chief, Big Foot Beach State Park contains 100 campsites and 1,900 feet of frontage on Geneva Lake. It's located within the city limits and is usually full on summer weekends. Call ahead for reservations. (414) 248-2528.

SUMMER EVENTS

Venetian Festival—A carnival, food booths and more, culminating in a lighted boat parade and fireworks. Held Wednesday through Sunday of the third weekend in August.

Concerts in the Park—Free concert series held in Flat Iron Park on Thursdays at 7 p.m. during July and August.

IN OTHER SEASONS

Oktoberfest—Arts and crafts, farmers' market, carriage rides and children's activities. Held Columbus Day weekend.

Christmas Parade—Downtown events, including a visit from Father Christmas. Held the first Saturday in December.

Ice-boating—Geneva Lake is considered one of three ice-boating "capitals" of the world. Boaters take to the lake as soon as conditions permit. Check with the Chamber of Commerce to see when competitions are scheduled. *For more information, contact the Geneva Lake Area Chamber of Commerce, (800) 345-1020.*

Mail carrier on the job.

DELIVERING THE MAIL

The postal service first offered lakeside mail delivery to homeowners on Geneva Lake in 1873, when wealthy Chicagoans began building their summer estates here. Since the estates were situated to take advantage of the setting, the public road was often a half-mile away, while the lake was right at the doorstep. Today, about 60 households receive their mail via the U.S. Mailboat Walworth II. It's as much a show as a service. The postal carriers are usually college students, out to earn some extra money from a summer job. Their task: to leap from the boat to the pier, slam in the mail, swoop up any outgoing mail, and hurtle back onto the boat. This all must take place in a period of about 10 seconds because the boat never stops, for fear wind would push it into the piers. There have been few missed jumps. (Carriers are auditioned for the job.) And the captain reports that "inadvertent" plunges into the lake rather suspiciously seem to occur on very hot days. ...

evening chills. Gemologists at Starfire Jewelry craft fine custom jewelry (wedding rings and remounts are a specialty). Allison Wonderland is packed with an array of imported toys, including fanciful cricket, frog, snake and dragonfly puppets. And if you like quality antiques, stop by Antiques International Ltd. and check out such things as an 1850s grandfather clock, Royal Doulton china and a massive English pub-style bar.

When you're wandering around town, be sure to stop by the Geneva Lake Area Museum of History at 818 Geneva St., where old photographs and displays show how things used to be. And when your feet are weary, rest in the public library at 918 Main St., a modernist structure designed by James P. Dresser, a student of Frank Lloyd Wright. The brocade-covered couches in the reading room are situated in front of broad picture windows, and offer one of the very best views of the shimmering lake.

IN THE AREA

For golfers, the Lake Geneva area is heaven on Earth. In addition to the golf courses at the Grand Geneva Resort & Spa, you'll find championship courses designed by Arnold Palmer and Lee Trevino (and a state-of-the-art golf academy) at Geneva National (414-245-7010) on Lake Como. Both courses are open to the public Monday through Thursday; they are open to the public on an alternating basis Friday through Sunday. The course at Abbey Springs in Fontana (414-275-6113) is reputed to be one of the prettiest in the state.

Horseback riding continues to be a Lake Geneva tradition. Saddle up a Tennessee walking horse at Keno Stable near Salem (414-537-2421) for a ride through the rolling, oak-forested countryside. The Kettle Moraine State Forest's southern unit (414-594-2135) contains 18,000 acres of beautiful glacial scenery, swimming beaches, a nature center and many miles of hiking trails. For a trip back to the 19th century, visit Old World Wisconsin, near Eagle (414-594-2116). Operated by the State Historical Society, the open-air museum features a collection of restored pioneer buildings, fields and gardens filled with old varieties of crops, and herds of rare breeds of animals. Guides dressed in period clothing act as interpreters.

Gardeners will want to stop by Northwind Perennial Farm (on Hospital Road, off Highway 120 north of Lake Geneva; 414-248-8229), which has an extensive demonstration garden, as well as a wide selection of native plants, perennials and ornamental grasses. If you're so inclined, you can place your bets on the greyhounds racing at Geneva Lakes Kennel Club in Delavan (800-477-4552). On Saturdays, stop by Williams Bay for a tour of the Yerkes Observatory (414-245-5555), the home of the world's largest refracting telescope. The 1897 facility, which is operated by the University of Chicago, still manufactures and tests state-of-the-art equipment. Evenings, the Belfry Theatre, Wisconsin's oldest summer stock playhouse, provides entertainment (414-245-0123). ▪

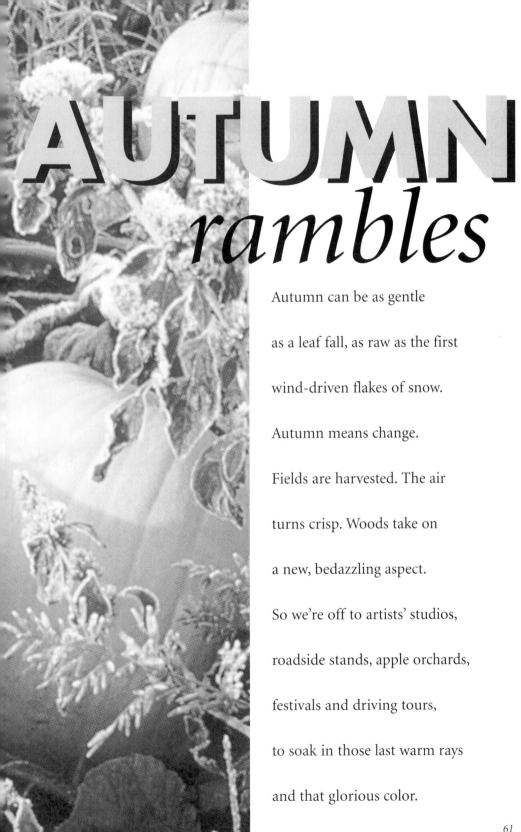

AUTUMN
rambles

Autumn can be as gentle

as a leaf fall, as raw as the first

wind-driven flakes of snow.

Autumn means change.

Fields are harvested. The air

turns crisp. Woods take on

a new, bedazzling aspect.

So we're off to artists' studios,

roadside stands, apple orchards,

festivals and driving tours,

to soak in those last warm rays

and that glorious color.

PICKS OF THE SEASON

september, october & november

1 TRAIN RIDE

ALL ABOARD FOR AUTUMN COLOR

There are almost as many ways to admire autumn's brilliant reds, oranges and yellows as there are leaves on Wisconsin trees. If you'd like a new angle, touring by train seldom disappoints.

In North Freedom, board an authentic turn-of-the-century Mid-Continent Steam Train and wind through the Baraboo River Valley past rock formations, open farmland and the ghost town of La Rue, once a mining oasis (800-22-DELLS or 800-930-1385). Edging the St. Croix River and Mississippi

Antique trains lead to colorful fall scenery.

River bluffs, the Osceola & St. Croix River Valley Railway is based at the historic 1916 Osceola Depot and uses vintage steam and diesel passenger equipment to re-create a mid-20th-century experience (800-643-7412). On the Kettle Moraine Scenic Steam Train, you'll chug eight miles through vibrant colors from North Lake to Merton (414-782-8074). Camp Five Museum in Laona offers a 20-minute train excursion and, upon debarkation, your choice of a guided ecology walk, the "Green Treasure Forest Tour" by guided surrey, or a pontoon-boat trip through a wildlife refuge (800-774-3414).

2 FESTIVAL

APPLE MANIA

Have a taste for apples? Then join the 40,000 apple lovers that descend on Bayfield the first weekend of October, when the town celebrates the harvest of this region's top crop.

All weekend you can indulge in an array of apple goodies, from caramel apples to apple pie, fritters and cider. Tour the orchards and take home a bushel or two of locally grown varieties. Saturday features an apple-peeling contest and a crafts fair. And on Sunday you can take in the Applefest parade and witness a unique rendition of "On

Wisconsin" by a 500-member marching band. For more information, call (800) 447-4094.

3 BICYCLING

OFF-ROAD AND UP NORTH

Northern Wisconsin, with its vast national and state forests, its miles of wooded logging roads and undulating trails, would seem a heaven on Earth for mountain

Off road in the Chequamegon.

bikers. But unless approved trails are mapped and marked, bikers tend to find themselves in the dark—as in, lost in the deep, dark woods.

Bikers, worry no more. The Chequamegon Area Mountain Biking Association (CAMBA) has mapped six clusters of trails in the Chequamegon National Forest. These offer a range of riding experiences to accommodate laid-back riders as well as thrill-seekers. All are

Festivities at Laura Ingalls Wilder Days.

well-marked and well worth riding, with eagles flying overhead and even an occasional wolf track imbedded in the path. Maps can be purchased in bike stores in the Hayward area. For more information, call (800) 533-7454, or e-mail gocable@win.bright.net.

4 DRIVING TOUR
AUTUMN SPLENDOR IN CABLE COUNTRY

A drive through northern woods exploding with color adds magic to any fall weekend. It's easy to pick the most colorful weekend and route in the Chequamegon National Forest—even if you live hundreds of miles from its bright poplar, maple and birch trees. Just call the Cable Area Chamber of Commerce at (800) 533-7454 to find out when the colors are at their most breathtaking.

The chamber can also provide a guidebook of three marked driving tours to take

you past scenic forests like the Porcupine Lake Wilderness Area. If you look closely you might even glimpse some of the area's shyest residents— deer, otter, bear and eagles.

5 FESTIVAL
WILDER DAYS

L aura Ingalls Wilder, author of *Little House on the Prairie* and other "Little House" books, was born in Pepin, a small town on the Mississippi River. To honor her work, Pepin hosts Laura Ingalls Wilder Days every September. The event features crafts of the mid-1800s, including blacksmithing, woodworking, weaving and quilting. You can listen to performances of songs and stories from Wilder's books, and kick up your heels at an old-time barn dance. And if you're a young girl between the ages of 4 and 10, enter the Laura Ingalls Wilder look-alike contest. For dates and details, call (715) 442-3011.

6 SHOPPING
HORSERADISH, OUR FIERY CROP

E llis Huntsinger was a lightning-rod salesman when he planted a half-acre of horseradish as a cash crop to get his family through the Depression. The plants thrived in Wisconsin's cool climate, and by the 1950s Huntsinger was growing tons of the fiery-hot root, which he mixed with good Wisconsin cream to create a flavorful condiment. His Silver Spring Gardens, near Eau Claire, is the largest producer of horseradish in the country. And its famous product can still make a grown man cry. Stop by Silver Spring Gardens, Highway 37 south of Eau Claire, for a jar. (715) 832-9739.

Free venison burgers at Tomahawk's Venison Feed.

7 FESTIVAL

VENISON FOR ALL

The town of Tomahawk likes to start the deer-hunting season off right—with a reminder of how tasty the outcome of the hunt really is. On the day before the gun-deer season opens, residents fire up the charcoal grills on main street and cook 3,000 venison burgers. The burgers, plus chips and soft drinks, are free at the Venison Feed. An added attraction: the Kiss-a-Pig Contest. Yes, a real pig is used, and the prize is, fittingly, a ham.

For dates and details, call the Tomahawk Chamber of Commerce at (800) 569-2160.

8 MUSEUM

BIRDS IN ART

The story of the Leigh Yawkey Woodson Art Museum's "Birds in Art" exhibit began decades ago, when the daughters of Wausau business-

Birds are the primary subject at the annual "Birds in Art" exhibit.

man Aytchmonde Woodson and his wife Leigh wanted to display their mother's collection of Royal Worcester porcelain birds, one of only seven complete sets in the world. Toward that end, family members donated a Tudor home for a museum, and Owen Gromme, wildlife painter and former curator of the Milwaukee Public Museum, was asked to plan an inaugural exhibit. Featuring the world's finest bird painters, carvers and sculptors, "Birds in Art" has since become an international event, touring to such far-flung places as Alaska, Honolulu, Peking, Stockholm, London and the Smithsonian in Washington, D.C. It starts, of course, at its home base, the Leigh Yawkey Woodson Art Museum in Wausau. The exhibit generally runs in September and October. Call (715) 845-7010 for exact dates.

Harry Houdini, inspiration for a magic convention.

9 FESTIVAL
HORSE & BUGGY DAYS

Nostalgic for the days of pioneers and horse-drawn carriages? Well, just grab your bonnet and head over to Weyauwega's Horse & Buggy Days, held annually on the second weekend in September. You'll find free buggy rides, an antique car and tractor parade, folks in period costume, a Civil War demonstration and performances by clowns, musical groups and square dancers. For dates and details, call (414) 867-2500.

10 CONVENTION
IT MUST BE MAGIC

Harry Houdini, people say, was the world's greatest magician, the man no fetter, no lock, no restraint could hold. Almost 70 years after his death, some of the methods behind his fantastic escapes are still mysteries. How fitting then that the Houdini Club of Wisconsin holds a magic convention—one of the leading gatherings of magicians in the country—in Oshkosh or Appleton, the town where Harry Houdini spent the early years of his life.

The convention, usually held on Labor Day weekend, features lectures, contests and dealer displays where registrants can select new tricks. The convention also includes public performances by professional entertainer-magicians. Call (414) 453-7018 for dates and schedules, or, in the Chicago area, call (708) 675-7801.

11 MUSEUM

GO, PACKERS!

The story is that, in 1927, after the National Football League made up its season game schedule, the owner of the New York team was somewhat puzzled by one of his matches. "Green Bay?" he inquired. "Where is Green Bay?" George Halas, the owner of the Chicago Bears at the time, responded easily. "After you play the team up there," Halas warned, "you'll know where Green Bay is."

What an accurate prophecy! The Green Bay Packers beat New York that fall; in 1929, '30 and '31 the Packers went on to win three National Football League championships. In the years since then the team has won more world championships than any other professional football team.

You can relive the high points of Packers history at a terrific facility set up in the team's honor: the Green Bay Packers Hall of Fame in Green Bay. Mural-size photos of famous players are marvelous, and film clips show all the best moments, as well as some hilarious "bloopers." You can even practice your own kicking

and passing in a special room set up with billboard instructions from the masters. The hall is located at 855 Lombardi Ave. Call (414) 499-4281 for hours.

12 DRIVING TOUR

DOOR COUNTY'S BELGIAN HERITAGE

Sometimes even the most interesting and knowledgeable of tour guides can talk so much it makes you wish for a "pause" button. We know of at least one guide who won't mind if you turn him off for a while: Jerry Guth, whose recorded voice narrates the Belgian Ethnic Tour, a self-guided cassette tour of Door, Kewaunee and Brown counties. A few "pauses" are required, Guth points out, not only for driving from place to place, but for pondering the rich heritage of this landscape.

Jerry will tell you about the old Belgian-settled communities of Champion, Dykesville, Euren, Rosiere, Brussels, Namur, Lincoln and Maplewood, all still home to high concentrations of Belgians. You'll hear songs sung in a language called Walloon, bits of legend and stories about interesting characters, like the first white man—a Belgian—to land in Wisconsin in 1634. You'll see Belgian chapels and shrines, and learn about Kermiss, the Belgian thanksgiving for a good harvest.

Packers Hall of Fame.

You can purchase the Wisconsin Belgian Ethnic Tour from area businesses or from the producer, Wisconsin's Ethnic Settlement Trail (W.E.S.T.). Call (414) 467-0636 or (414) 961-2110 in the Milwaukee Metro Area, for ordering information. Tapes are also available for a Dutch tour, in Brown and Outagamie counties, and a Czech tour, in Manitowoc and Kewaunee counties. Tours of other ethnic settlement areas are in the works.

Belgian summer kitchen.

13 FESTIVAL

THE OLDEST OKTOBERFEST

It all started long ago in a faraway land, when Bavarian Crown Prince Ludwig took the Princess Therese as his bride. The year was 1810 and the wedding was held in a meadow. An accompanying celebration of the harvest was such a hit that a yearly festival, called the "Trachtenfest," has been held ever since in this same clearing, now surrounded by the concrete buildings of Munich. From the Trachtenfest, came the inspiration for La Crosse's "Oktoberfest U.S.A."— one of the oldest Oktoberfests in the nation.

The festival is as merry a scene as the original. The purpose is the same too: to celebrate the season's harvest and to enjoy food, drink and laughter with good friends. In addition to the famous street party, there's a whirl of events to choose from throughout the week. Rock 'n' roll, country-western and oldies bands are among the musical attractions, and what would Oktoberfest be without the rollicking *oompahs* of the polka? All kinds of arts and crafts are on display, and a food fair serves up brats, kielbasa, beer and other assorted Wisconsin delicacies. It all takes place at the Oktoberfest grounds, adjacent to Riverside Park and at Copeland Park on the La Crosse riverfront. Call (608) 784-FEST for details.

14 DRIVING TOUR

CRANBERRY COUNTRY

One visit to Warrens, the self-proclaimed cranberry capital of Wisconsin, and you'll never take this tart little berry for granted. Warrens'

2,000 acres of cranberry marshes—the largest concentration in the state—makes cranberries the top attraction in this town in northeastern Monroe County.

A good way to see the cranberry marshes is by driving or biking along one of three routes mapped out for visitors. Try the 23-mile Wetlands Tour for the best view of the marshes. On the same tour you'll see where sphagnum moss—another important local crop —is harvested for eventual use in the florist industry. For cranberry history and trivia, stop by the Cranberry Expo Ltd., which boasts the world's largest cranberry museum and is operated by the Clinton Potter family, fifth-generation cranberry growers. While you're there, sample cranberry ice cream, juice and pie.

If you plan a trip to Warrens during Cranberry Festival (held in late September), leave your bike at home—organizers say the area is too congested during the event for safe riding. But other treats this weekend include harvest tours, a carnival, and an arts and crafts show. For a schedule of events or for more information on group tours call (608) 372-2166.

15 NATURE

WINGS OVER PETENWELL

Catch waterfowl activity at its peak with a fall visit to the Petenwell Wildlife Area in

Harvesting cranberries.

Waterfowl flock to Petenwell Wildlife Area.

Adams County, directly adjacent to the Wisconsin River just east of Necedah. A stroll around the area's four ponds will yield sightings of common mergansers, blue-winged teal, Canada geese and black ducks. Hike the 2.7-mile trail and watch for ospreys, eagles, sandhill cranes, herons and maybe a least bittern. If you're lucky a Blanding's turtle, an endangered species, will be sunning itself along the water's edge.

Located along the shores of Petenwell Flowage, Wisconsin's second-largest lake, the wildlife area is comprised of 270 acres of wetlands, marsh, speckled alder swamps, and oak and aspen woods. Early fall is the best time to visit this spectacular wildlife area; it closes down from October 1 until the end of April due to eagle nesting. For more information, call (715) 422-3927.

Artist at work, Mineral Point.

Apples by the bushel at Gibbsville Orchard.

16 ARTS

VISIT SOUTHWEST ARTISTS IN ACTION

The Baraboo Hills are alive with the sound of ... metal being soldered, glass being blown, and wood being carved. Artists there (and in Spring Green and Mineral Point) are busy at work making beautiful objects.

In October you can catch them in the act during the Fall Art Tour, an annual weekend when two dozen of southwest Wisconsin's premier talents—painters, sculptors, potters, weavers, goldsmiths and mixed-media artists—throw open their doors and let in the public for an intimate look at how their works are made. Part of the fun is getting to view the private environments in which each artist does his or her thing. Another part is rambling through this region's breathtaking countryside.

For exact dates and a map of the current year's tour, call the chamber of commerce in Mineral Point (608-987-3201), Spring Green (608-588-2042; 800-588-2042), or Baraboo (800-227-2266).

17 ORCHARD

HERITAGE APPLES

When your taste buds yearn for something a little sweeter, more winey or more tart than McIntosh or Delicious, head for the Gibbsville Orchard in Gibbsville. Here you can sample 36 varieties of apples, including some old ones that you might never have heard of but that your great-grandparents probably loved. Among the many choices are Russet, Wolf River, Snow, Winesap and Yellow Transparent. The orchard also sells award-winning cider—bring your own jugs and fill 'em up at the spigot. Also available are Flemish pears, tart cherries and plums. Gibbsville Orchard is located on Highway 32. Call (414) 564-2944 for more information.

Making dinner the old-fashioned way.

18 EVENT

GREENBUSH HARVEST DINNERS

In the 1850s, stagecoach travelers passing between Sheboygan and Fond du Lac could always count on a hearty meal at the Wade House in Greenbush. Modern-day visitors can too, but they should be prepared to roll up their sleeves and work for it. On weekends in November, the historic inn, operated by the State Historical Society, holds a series of harvest dinners. Each dinner guest travels back in time to help turn out a traditional harvest meal, and is charged with a particular task. But there are no microwaves or toasters here; instead, you'll use the implements of a bygone era, a woodburning stove and an open-hearth fire. So popular are the dinners that you must reserve a place at the table at least five months in advance. Call (414) 526-3271.

19 FESTIVAL

FABULOUS FUNGI

The first thing you notice as you head down the second-floor passageway in the Milwaukee Public Museum toward the site of the annual Mushroom Fair is not the colorful arrangement of mushroom photographs that lines the walls. Nor is it the mushroom face-painting booth, where young children's faces are adorned with surprisingly

Celebrate—and sample—mushrooms at Milwaukee's Mushroom Fair.

your neighborhood, you can bring it in to be identified and discussed by experts.

The fair is usually held in September. For more information, call (414) 278-2700.

20 EVENT

KENOSHA'S DANISH BREAKFAST

A rich and tantalizing aroma fills Kenosha's historic Danish Brotherhood Lodge during its annual Danish breakfast, usually held the second weekend in November. Hundreds line up bright and early for a taste of the authentic Old World cuisine—and they are quickly rewarded with generous servings of *aebleskiver*, Danish ball-shaped pancakes; locally made *medisterpolse*, or Danish sausage; and buttery pecan or fruit-filled kringle from Racine's O & H Bakery.

Kenosha lays claim to the largest Danish Brotherhood in the United States, 400 members. You'll find the Lodge at 2206 63rd St. in Kenosha. Call (414) 657-9781 or (414) 657-3895.

good likenesses of *Amanita muscaria*. No, the first thing you notice is the odor—a dense, musky scent reminiscent of a walk in the woods on a damp day.

What you are smelling, of course, is mushrooms, hundreds of them lovingly harvested a day earlier by members of the Wisconsin Mycological Society, sponsors of the fair. Visitors here enjoy mushrooms in a multitude of ways: You can sample mushroom dishes, view mushroom movies, go for a mushroom hunt throughout the museum, and attend slide shows and lectures. If you've found a mystery mushroom in

weekend **ADVENTURES**

Look for artistic treasures in historic Mineral Point, discover the lost-in-time village of Rural, and watch one of nature's greatest spectacles, when hundreds of thousands of geese gather at Horicon Marsh.

RURAL ▲

HORICON MARSH ▲

MINERAL POINT ▲

73

MINERAL POINT

*Mineral Point,
Where Art
Meets History*

R idgetop highways in
southwest Wisconsin
sweep past valleys
hidden below. Travelers on the
main roads can easily miss
farms nestled on wooded hillsides, creeks snaking along the
bottomlands and, in the case of
Mineral Point, a village rich in
history. But turn off Highway
151 at a small green sign pro-
claiming "Historic District,"
and you will follow a street
that descends into a downtown
that looks much as it did in
the 1800s.

The settlement was estab-
lished by prospectors in 1827
(in those days, lead was
referred to as "mineral"), and
word soon spread to Cornwall,
England, that fortunes could
be made here. Cornish miners
arrived in a steady stream, and

Pendarvis Historic Site.

in 1829 Mineral Point was named as the county seat of Iowa County, in what was then Michigan Territory, which included all of southwestern Wisconsin. The town prospered as a mining and political center until 1848, when news of gold in California lured area miners to a new promised land. Although zinc mining provided a second boom in the late 1890s, the Depression hit Mineral Point hard. It settled into a quiet decline until the mid-1930s, when historic renovation brought new settlers, and new life, to town.

Mineral Point's renaissance is credited to Robert Neal and Edgar Hellum who, in 1935, purchased a century-old, decrepit stone building on Shake Rag Street for $10 in back taxes. The pair carefully rebuilt the structure, christened it Pendarvis House, and eventually opened a restaurant, serving traditional Cornish foods. Over the years, Neal and Hellum restored a home next door for themselves, and a group of row houses on the hill above.

In 1940, Milwaukee artists Max and Ava Fernekes were headed to Galena on a sketching trip when they stopped at Pendarvis House for dinner. The couple fell in love with the town and moved to Mineral Point shortly after, determined to make a living selling their sculptures and watercolors. As Neal and Hellum created the impetus for historic renovation in town, the Fernekes set the stage for an influx of artists. Today Mineral Point is a true artists' colony, with more than 20 shops and galleries owned by artists-in-residence.

Antique Fair and Encampment at the Gundry House Museum.

THE TOWN

All of Mineral Point is designated a historic district and its streets—many steep and narrow, following the wandering footpaths of miners—are lined with fine homes, storefronts and cottages. You'll quickly notice the extensive use of limestone. The Cornish built few log houses since wood was needed as fuel for smelters. Skilled stonecutters and masons, they were able to take advantage of Mineral Point's limestone, which could be quarried on the spot. Today, their little stone buildings give the community its distinctive charm.

Lead miner re-enactor describes his trade.

Begin your visit with a trip to Pendarvis, now operated by the State Historical Society as Pendarvis Historic Site. Here, Mineral Point's history comes alive, recalled by a costumed guide who explains the mining displays and authentic furnishings. Call (608) 987-2122 for tour times. Across the street a network of walking

trails crisscross the hillside, leading visitors past the crevice mines and badger holes of the Merry Christmas Mine.

Then head downtown to Mineral Point's diverse array of shops and galleries. There are dozens to explore. At Against the Grain Woodworks, 31 High St., Don Mahieu carves hardwoods and burls into fish, frogs and leaves. Some pieces are offered in number; others are one-of-a-kind conceptual sculptures, like the frog squatting inside the door with an extended tongue wrapped around his dinner. Johnston Gallery, 245 High St., showcases fanciful wood pieces, jewelry, finely wrought pewterware and other works by 120 artists, including slab-built porcelain and stoneware created by owners Tom and Diana Johnston.

The scatter rugs, wall hangings and clothing in Studio on High, 154 High St., intrigue shoppers with their texture as much as with their fiber and color. Owner/weaver Sue John will gladly explain the subtleties, pointing to her own rugs of Scandinavian design in progress on two looms in the back of her store. Glass works draw visitors into Sirius Sunlight, 218 High St. Jill Engels, the only native-born artist in town, creates two- and three-dimensional stained-glass pieces, while her partner, Chuck Pound, concentrates on "aquariphernalia": glass

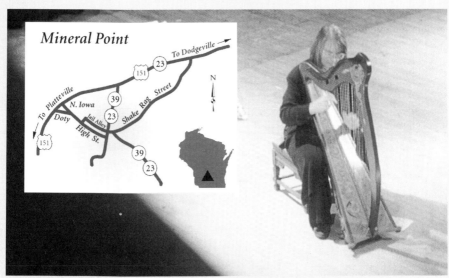

Performance at the Mineral Point Opera House.

EATING WELL

Chesterfield Inn—Enjoy lunch and dinner—the menu includes steak, fish, homemade pasta and choice desserts—in a renovated historic building. 20 Commerce St. (608) 987-3682.

Pointer Cafe—Family dining with an activity area for children. Highway 151 South. (608) 987-3733.

Red Rooster Cafe—A town fixture, conveniently located, with solid cafe fare, along with pasties, figgy hobbin and bread pudding. 158 High St. (608) 987-9936.

Redwood Family Restaurant—Breakfast and lunch are served in a friendly atmosphere. Try Aunt Cora's delicious homemade Cornish pasty. Highway 151. (608) 987-2242.

Royal Inn—A local favorite for steaks, Friday fish fry, Saturday prime rib and, occasionally, catfish and grilled salmon. 43 High St. (608) 987-3051.

Sweet Shoppe—Need a break from shopping? Stop here for coffee and a pastry, a root beer float or sandwich. 60 High St. (608) 987-3961.

LODGING

Cothren House—This elegant stone family estate was built in 1853 and includes two acres of landscaped grounds with formal gardens, a croquet court and garden gazebo. Lodging options: bedrooms in the main house, a restored 1835 log cabin or a two-bedroom guest house. (608) 987-2612.

Knudson's Guest House—Relax in this restored brick home in Mineral Point's residential area. (608) 987-2733.

Wm. A. Jones House—Built in 1906 by the U.S. Commissioner of Indian Affairs, the Jones House features original woodwork and seven tiled fireplaces. (608) 987-2337.

Wilson House Inn—This 1853 home offers four bedrooms, some with private bath. Sample small-town living from the vantage point of the front-porch swing. (608) 987-3600.

AUTUMN EVENTS

Cornish Festival—Bus tours of the historic district, performers, a pasty banquet, an old-fashioned Fair on the Green and Taste of Mineral Point. Held the last weekend in September.

Mineral Point Real Antiques Show—More than 30 dealers exhibit their wares at the Iowa County Fairgrounds. Held mid-October (also held in June).

Fall Art Tour—Artists in Mineral Point, Spring Green and Baraboo open their studios to the public. Pick up maps for the Mineral Point tour at the Johnston Gallery, 245 High St. Held the third weekend in October.

IN OTHER SEASONS

Territory Days—Celebrate the Fourth of July with a parade, running race, chicken barbeque, city band concerts and fireworks at dusk.

Mineral Point Art Festival—Juried art show with entertainment and refreshments. Held in August.

For more information, contact the Mineral Point Chamber of Commerce, (608) 987-3201.

angelfish, bubbles and plants gently floating in aquariums. At her scent-filled shop, 234 High St., Robin Cahill specializes in dried arrangements, hard-to-find herb plants in season and one-of-a-kind antiques.

Three ceramic artists have

Fine antiques catch the eye.

storefronts on Commerce Street. Frank Polizzi of Mulberry Pottery utilizes local raw materials for his pots, and fires them in a wood-burning kiln. An enormous, smiling ceramic pig greets you inside the door of Howdle Studio, where Bruce Howdle creates functional ware as well as hand-built sculptures and commissioned relief murals. Harriet Story, owner of Story Pottery, focuses on wheel-thrown tableware in muted earth colors, but also throws wall pieces and installations

inspired by the designs of African and South American cultures. Here, too, are baskets, jewelry, twig furniture and wooden bowls from artists around the country.

On Jail Alley, the location of Mineral Point's original jail, sits Jail Alley House Gallery, the oldest gallery in town. Its first floor is filled with kitchenware, furniture, quilts and figurines. The lower level houses Paper Mountain Books, with fondly remembered children's titles, used and out-of-print books, toy soldiers and old sheet music. Look for Jean and Bert Bohlin's needleart and fine wood pieces at nearby Needlewood, located in a lovely restored brick home.

Appropriately, antique dealers figure as prominently in Mineral Point as artists. A half-dozen or so shops contain the whole range of vintage accessories and furnishings, from delicate table linens to elaborate Victorian bed frames. Some of these are open year-round, others by chance or appointment, but you can count on them all being open from May through October. Search for Wisconsin history at Foundry Books, 105 Commerce St., which specializes in out-of-print books, maps and documents about Wisconsin's past. Or sample local wine at Mineral Springs Winery at the far end of Shake Rag Street. Peg and Bob Borucki make

11 wines on the premises of the original Mineral Springs Brewery, and visitors may taste them all for free.

For an overview of architectural and historic points of interest, pick up a brochure from the Visitors Bureau, 225 High St., that describes a self-guided driving tour. Byrne Livery offers narrated tours in a horse-drawn carriage by reservation; call (608) 987-2692.

IN THE AREA

A short drive north from Mineral Point on Highway 23, Governor Dodge State Park offers more than 5,000 acres of tree-covered hills and valleys. The Stephens Falls Hiking Trail, a short one-quarter mile, leads walkers through the woods to a hidden waterfall and stream. For spectacular color, take the 4.5-mile White Oak Trail, which winds around Cox Hollow Lake and climbs up steep, rocky grades. The park also contains two lakes with swimming beaches, boating access, picnic areas and more than 200 campsites. Call (608) 935-2315 for more information.

Blackhawk Lake Recreation Area, a lovely little-known spot, features a clear lake with beach and boat access. It's located north of Cobb on County BH (608-623-2707). In Platteville, you can take a trip underground into a restored lead mine at the Platteville Mining Museum, 405 E. Main St. ∎

CORNISH PASTIES

Legend says that a well-made Cornish pasty could be dropped down a mine shaft and not break a-part. Here is the recipe used by Robert Neal for the pasties he served in his dining room at Pendarvis during the '30s and '40s. We haven't tested its "droppa-bility," but you'll find it to be good, solid fare.

CRUST:
3 cups all-purpose flour
1 1/2 teaspoons salt
2/3 cup shortening
1/4 to 1/3 cup water
1/2 teaspoon baking powder (if a lighter crust
   is desired)

Sift together flour, salt and baking powder, if desired. Cut in shortening. Add enough water for the dough to hold together. Roll dough out into a circle, and place on a cookie sheet or shallow pan.

FILLING:
2 pounds round steak
3/4 cup coarsely chopped onion
3 cups raw potatoes, thinly sliced
1/4 cup suet, ground or cut in small pieces
1 scant tablespoon salt
1/2 teaspoon pepper
Small amount of rutabagas or carrots (if desired)

Cut the tough parts from the meat and slice it into 1/2-inch cubes. Mix with onions, potatoes, suet, salt and pepper. Put the mixture on half the circle of pastry and fold it over, as you would a turnover. Pinch the edge and fold it over to resemble a seam. Make small, three-cornered openings in the crust about three inches apart. Bake in 350-degree oven for 1 1/2 hours. (After a half hour of baking, pour a little cream into each opening to make the pasty juicy; this may be done a couple of times during the baking.) Serves four to six.

RURAL

Rural,
The Town That
Time Forgot

Come October, the eye
yearns for the arche-
typal autumn scene:
a bushel of apples crisp and
pungent, pumpkins grown to
astonishing proportions and
deep-yellow maple trees set off
by a pure-white house. That's
when it's time to visit Rural in
Waupaca County. Yankees
came here in the 1850s and
built what felt like home—a
classic New England town
among the hardwoods and the
winding, burbling Crystal
River. For 20 years Rural
boomed, the site of a prosper-
ous mill, lumber company, dry
goods store, even a millinery
shop. Then the railroad passed
the village by. Time seemed to
ignore it as well. Today, tiny
Rural is one of only two communities in the state (Rock
County's Cooksville is the
other) that, 140 years after settlement, retains its Yankee pioneer character, with still-lived-
in homes of white clapboard
and black shutters and a personality so serene visitors feel
as if they've stepped back into
the 19th century.

Crystal River Inn.

A moment out of history in the Rural cemetery.

THE VILLAGE

One of Rural's favorite tales is of resident Tom Potts, who, 70 or so years ago, was disturbed by the rush of new-fangled motor cars and one day hauled his rocking chair into the road to slow everybody down. Rural is still best toured on foot—there's so little traffic you can walk, unconcerned, down the middle of the street. An expedition around the two-block-by-three-block village can take only half an hour, but plan on considerably longer since you'll want to gaze often into the crystal-clear Crystal River and admire the stately homes.

You'll find that much of old Rural is gone, including the school, church and mill (the latter built by founder James Hinchman Jones, a Welsh entrepreneur who called the area his "rural holdings"). But 13 houses listed on the National Register of Historic Places remain. Ironically, Rural's failure to thrive saved its architecture; residents simply could not afford to make "improvements." When preservation-minded families purchased properties in the '70s and '80s, they found structures that hardly had changed over the course of a century.

With one exception (the Italianate Radley House), Rural's architecture is all Greek Revival, square and spare, handsome and dignified, without the curlicues and gingerbread that adorn Victorian homes built later in the century. Such a large assembly of well-kept early architecture is rare in Wisconsin. The great joy of strolling around Rural is simply looking at these gracious buildings and noticing the subtle half-columns, the tall windows, the doorway fans and other finely wrought architectural details. Pick up the Rural Historical Society's brochure, "Tour of Historic Sites in Rural," at the Crystal River Inn or Halfway House Antiques, both on Rural Road, to guide you around.

Rural has no organized "attractions," but there are a couple of stopping-off points to keep your walk slow and leisurely. Weller's Store is one, primarily because of its 25-cent ice-cream cones. Another is the small building next to it with the tall false front, built in1898. The first Rural store, it now houses Rural Artists, a shop offering country gift items and colorful quilts. Up the street and around the corner on Rural Road, Halfway House Antiques sells antique pine furniture, pitchforks, sleds and other quality items. The small shop, run by Rural Historical Society president Jo Yaeger, is attached to Rural's oldest house, a stagecoach inn built by J. H. Jones in 1852. Farther down Rural Road, tucked into a bend of the river, sits the second home to be built in Rural, the 1853 An-

drew Potts House. Snowy white with green shutters and trim, it's now the Crystal River Inn, an idyllically situated bed and breakfast accommodation run by Lois and Gene Sorenson. If you can, book yourself into a room here. The inn's wooden Adirondack chairs, gazebo, screened-in porch and sun room provide some of the village's best vantage points. You'll discover that it's perfectly satisfying to sit here for hours listening to the murmuring of the river, the rustle of dry autumn leaves and the soft chatter of neighbors. A mowed path around the massive barn leads up a hill to the pioneer cemetery, where Rural's settlers look down, we're sure, with everlasting approval on their beautiful town.

IN THE AREA

When the trees blaze with color and the air smells of wood smoke, you'll want to be outdoors. Nearby Hartman Creek State Park (715-258-2372) offers 14 miles of delightful hiking trails. The one-mile Deer Path Trail around Allen Lake is especially scenic in fall, running through red pines, colorful oaks and maples, and a grove of golden hip-high ferns. For a longer trek, consider walking a section of the Ice Age Trail, which traverses an oak forest in the park, along the glacier's terminal moraine.

Paddlers can rent canoes at

Horse-drawn wagons transport visitors for Rural's house tour.

EATING WELL

Carnegie's—Located in the old public library building, this bright and airy restaurant serves excellent gourmet pastas and southwestern fare. Stellar desserts, too. 321 S. Main St. (715) 256-1031.

Crystal Cafe—About 17 miles north of Rural in Iola but worth the drive, the Crystal is famous for Wisconsin cafe food made fresh and from scratch. It's open 5:30 a.m. to 8 p.m. (715) 445-9227.

Wheelhouse Restaurant—Both locals and tourists favor the pizza here, generously sized and served overlooking the water in the heart of the Chain O'Lakes on County Q. (715) 258-8289.

King's Table—A King institution, this family restaurant serves jumbo cinnamon rolls, broasted chicken and Mexican specialties. County QQ. (715) 258-9150.

Clear Water Harbor—Charbroiled sandwiches, burgers and Sprecher's draft root beer are on the menu of this harborside restaurant, which features an open deck. Open through early October. County QQ in King. (715) 258-2866.

LODGING

Crystal River Inn—Rural's stellar (and only) bed and breakfast inn offers luxurious, relaxed comfort in a bucolic setting. Most rooms

have private baths; some contain fireplaces. (715) 258-5333.

Thomas Pipe Inn—Near Amherst about 13 miles northwest of Rural, the Thomas Pipe is an elegant B&B in a restored 1855 Greek Revival home. (715) 824-3161.

Grand Seasons—This 90-unit Best Western hotel in Waupaca features a fitness center, pool, whirlpool and sauna. (715) 258-9212.

Village Inn—This Waupaca motel offers lower-cost lodging in its older units; upgraded poolside rooms are available in the new wing. (715) 258-8526.

FALL EVENTS

Rural House Walk—For a rare

glimpse inside some of Rural's historic homes, attend the village's House Walk. It's usually held in September, but organizers occasionally skip a year, so call ahead.

Fall-O-Rama—The third weekend in September, Waupaca celebrates fall with a large arts and crafts fair, food and live entertainment.

IN OTHER SEASONS

Strawberry Festival—The longest strawberry shortcake, costume contest, arts and crafts, and more. Held the third weekend in June. *For more information, contact the Waupaca Area Chamber of Commerce, (800) 236-2222.*

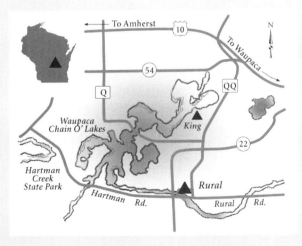

Ding's Dock on County Q
(800-236-7577 or 715-258-
2612) to navigate the chain of
22 lakes—some of the clearest,
cleanest water in the state—
from which the Crystal River
flows. You can also rent smaller,
fiberglass canoes here to take
you down the shallow Crystal
(by reservation only after Labor
Day). Kids especially love this
jaunt, which always includes a
few dumps due to the fast-flow-
ing river's rocks and curves.
Feeling less brave? Ride through
the chain on the Chief
Waupaca, a 60-foot sternwheel-
er offering tours from Clear
Water Harbor on County QQ
in King weekends through early
October (715-258-2866).

But what is fall without a
drive through a world turned
scarlet, orange, tawny and
bronze? From Rural turn your
car west down wooded Rustic
Road 23 (Hartman Road) past
more historic Yankee homes.
Jog north on Hartman Creek
Road to Highway 54 and turn
west for a visit to Turner's
Farm Market, resplendent with
pumpkins, Indian corn, gourds
and chrysanthemums. Then
head north and west on Nelson
Road and county highways K,
Q and B through Amish country to Amherst, a well-kept
small town with a terrific bakery (Pauc's Bakery—try the
apple-walnut and cheese-pep-
per breads), a wonderful quilting supply shop and Real
Goods/Snow-Belt Energy, an

alternative-energy store that
sells solar panels, wind
machines and all sorts of fascinating devices. From Amherst
drive east on County B to
Scandinavia, where Adeline's
Main Street Antiques features
vintage Coca-Cola bottles,
Wyatt Earp 45s, Wiley Coyote
glassware and other '50s
memorabilia. A detour north
on Highway 49 is a must: In
Iola, the Crystal Cafe will fill
you up with thick soups, sandwiches made with 1-inch slabs
of homemade bread, and pies
that rank among the best in
the state.

After backtracking to
Scandinavia, you are faced with
two tantalizing choices. Drive
west on County V and south
on Peterson Road and you will
come to Smokey Valley Road,
as delightful in fall as its name
implies, and Oakland Road,
which tunnels under a canopy
of bright yellow maple leaves.
Head east and south on Elm
Valley Road instead, and you'll
follow a branch of the Little
Wolf River past fields and
woods that blend every shade
of red, umber and gold. Either
way is a delight to the senses.

If you're looking for indoor
diversion, the Wilderness Print
Gallery, west of Rural on
Cleghorn Road, features the
work of 50 artists. Nearby Waupaca and King harbor numerous antique and gift shops, as
do Wild Rose and Wautoma a
little farther afield. ■

Enjoy some of the state's nicest back-roads bicycling.

BICYCLING WAUPACA COUNTY

To many eyes, Waupaca County bears a close resemblance to Ireland's Killarny: a wet, vibrantly green landscape dotted with small, shallow lakes. The terrain is gently rolling and the back roads lightly traveled. Combined with the scenery, this makes for some of the nicest bicycling in the state.

To help bicyclists find their way around, the county Parks and Recreation Department has put together a book of bicycle routes ranging from 15 to 60 miles in length and starting from various small towns. In addition, the rangers at Hartman Creek State Park have plotted routes of one to seven miles starting from the park. They also provide maps of the local metric-century ride, which consists of three loops of 15, 23 and 24 miles. All maps are available at the park office, west of Rural on Hartman Creek Road.

HORICON MARSH

The Spectacle of the Geese at Horicon Marsh

At first, they're indistinct, nothing more than a smudge on the horizon. But when the flock resolves into focus, there is no mistaking the undulating V. Another flock is spotted, and another, and another, until at last the sky is alive with birds. The air reverberates to their brassy clangor.

The geese are back at Horicon Marsh. In spring, they undertook a long, hazardous migration to nesting grounds at Hudson Bay. There, they fiercely protected their young from predators, and after the downy goslings were fully

Hundreds of thousands of geese stop over on their long fly south.

grown and capable of flight, just two months after pipping out of their shells, the family headed south. Every autumn, several hundred thousand of them stop at Dodge County's Horicon Marsh and the area surrounding it before resuming the southward migration. The sight of these huge flocks of Canada geese, swarming out of the marsh at dawn on their daily feeding flight or returning at dusk, is one of the most magnificent wildlife spectacles on Earth.

But while today the 32,000-acre, 13½-mile-long by 5½-mile-wide Horicon Marsh is virtually synonymous with Canada geese, this wasn't always the case. In fact, geese were historically considered something of a rarity in the area.

In the 19th century, Horicon was famed, instead, as a paradise for other forms of wildlife. It offered some of the finest duck hunting in the Midwest. The marsh hay meadows were filled with flocks of prairie chicken. Muskrats were so numerous that upward of 100,000 pelts could be taken every year without denting the population. Northern pike grew to enormous sizes in the marsh's fertile waters, heavy-bellied bass were common, perch averaged a pound apiece. So many bullfrogs were shipped to Milwaukee restaurants that the market was flooded.

Then, in the early 1900s, a group of investors led by a Chicago financier concocted a scheme to drain the marsh and sell it off as farmland. They even distributed a pamphlet that described Horicon as a potential Eden for the growing

Visitors observe birds from trails and a scenic drive.

of root crops. Sportsmen's clubs adamantly opposed the project; the Wisconsin Supreme Court ruled against it. But the developers heeded no voice save that of their own greed. Between 1910 and 1916, an extensive network of drainage ditches was gouged out of the marsh. The plows followed the dredges and, as promised, vegetables grew robustly in the rich organic soil. A bitter surprise, however, lay in store at harvest time. The crops had a pronounced "peaty" flavor, which might be desirable in Scotch whisky but not in onions, carrots and potatoes.

This revelation, combined with the fact that the marsh, despite the best (or worst) efforts of the drainage engineers, was often still saturated with water, put the farmers out of business in a hurry. They left behind a wasteland, as useless to wildlife as it had been to agriculture. Symbolic of the devastation, some of the exposed peat dried, caught fire, and continued to burn intermittently for 12 years. Blanketed by clouds of acrid smoke, once-great Horicon Marsh resembled nothing so much as a charred World War I battlefield.

Fortunately, a handful of conservationists fervently believed that Horicon could be great again, and in 1921 they began to lobby for its restoration. The Wisconsin Legislature passed the Horicon Marsh Wildlife Refuge Bill in 1927, and a dam to regulate water levels was completed in 1934. As the waters rose, filling the basin of this ancient glacial lake, aquatic vegetation and the wildlife dependent on it

returned more swiftly than anyone dared hope. Horicon Marsh became the first, and remains one of the best, examples of a phenomenon that has since been demonstrated repeatedly: Given half a chance, nature heals itself.

With the establishment of the 21,000-acre Horicon National Wildlife Refuge in 1941 (the 11,000-acre, state-owned Horicon Marsh Wildlife Area was by then already in place), the marsh was once again whole. The geese discovered it shortly thereafter. From a trickle of honkers in the mid-'40s, their numbers increased to 51,000 in 1958. That figure quadrupled by the early '70s, and it would have grown even higher if the DNR hadn't "spread out" the flock by restoring other prime marshes in the east-central part of the state.

The geese have plenty of company. All told, 264 species of birds have been identified here, including several—great egret, Forster's tern, bald eagle, peregrine falcon—that are on Wisconsin's threatened and endangered species lists. The great egret rookery on Horicon's Fourmile Island (itself a natural area) is the largest in Wisconsin. Many mammals and fish call Horicon home as well. It's little wonder that, in 1991, Horicon was designated a "Wetland of International Importance" by a global panel of ecologists.

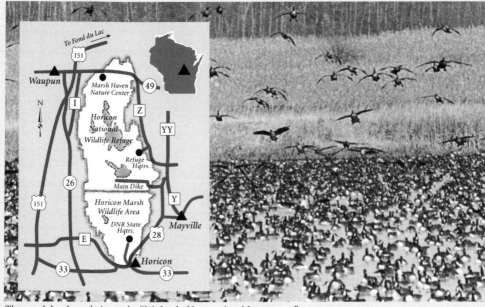

The marsh has been designated a "Wetland of International Importance."

EATING WELL

Helen's Kitchen—Sample the broasted chicken and homemade pies. 1116 W. Main St., Waupun. (414) 324-3441.

Hopp's Restaurant—Made-from-scratch pizza draws locals to this family restaurant. 5 W. Main St., Waupun. (414) 324-4251.

Audubon Inn—Fine fare is served for lunch and dinner on weekends (dinner only during the week) in a historic building. 45 N. Main St., Mayville. (414) 387-5858.

Schreiner's—This popular family restaurant features delectable comfort food. Try the chicken and dumplings or the hearty ham loaf. 168 N. Pioneer Rd., Fond du Lac. (414) 922-0590.

LODGING

Rose Ivy Inn—A romantic Queen Anne home in Waupun with breakfast served, on warm mornings, in a glass-enclosed porch. (414) 324-2127.

Audubon Inn—This restored 1896 hotel in Mayville, listed on the National Register of Historic Places, pampers guests with double whirlpools and handmade quilts. (414) 387-5858.

Mayville Inn—A new, quaint and cozy family-run inn, in Mayville, with 29 rooms. (414) 387-1234.

J & R's Sherm-Inn—This 1872 Cream City brick farmhouse, in Mayville, is now a bed and breakfast inn with two rooms. (414) 387-4642.

Holiday Inn Holidome—The full range of motel services, including an indoor pool, sauna, whirlpool and adjacent golf course, in Fond du Lac. (414) 923-1440; (800) HOLIDAY.

AUTUMN EVENTS

German Volksfest—Ethnic food, crafts and entertainment. Held in downtown Waupun in September.
Art on the Marsh—Painters, sculptors, woodcarvers and craftspeople from throughout the Midwest display nature-inspired work at Discher Park in Horicon. Held in September.
Audubon Days—A parade, bed race, decorated scarecrow competition, bike and bus tours of the marsh, polka contest and more. Held in Mayville the first weekend in October.

IN OTHER SEASONS

Klompenfest—Waupun honors its Dutch heritage with wooden-shoe carving, entertainment and ethnic foods. Held in June.
Horicon Marsh Days—Community festival with parade and carnival. Held in July.
Tour de Marsh—Fifty-mile bike ride sponsored by Waupun Jaycees. Held in August.
For more information, contact the Horicon Chamber of Commerce, (414) 485-3200; the Mayville Chamber of Commerce, (414) 387-5776; the Waupun Chamber of Commerce, (414) 324-3491; and the Fond du Lac Convention & Visitors Bureau, (414) 923-3010.

A V formation makes flying easier.

GEESE IN FLIGHT

Canada geese typically fly 40 to 50 miles an hour, and with the aid of a tail wind can easily travel 70 miles an hour. That enables them to cover the 850 miles between Hudson Bay and Horicon Marsh in 12 to 15 hours. After leaving Horicon, the geese embark on an additional seven- to 10-hour flight to wintering grounds in southern Illinois.

During these long-distance treks, the geese fly in a V formation, apparently to reduce wind resistance. To take advantage of favorable winds, they may course the sky at extremely high altitudes. Whereas geese normally ascend only up to 500 feet, migrating geese gain, on average, 2,000 to 3,000 feet in altitude, and have been observed flying as high as 10,000 feet.

VIEWING THE MARSH

When the geese are "in"— they start arriving about mid-September—you can literally drive anywhere in the vicinity of Horicon Marsh and see them. The best auto tour route, however, is the 36-mile Wild Goose Parkway. Beginning on County E just west of the city of Horicon, the parkway (watch for signs) completely circumnavigates the marsh. For a panoramic vista of this vast, sprawling wetland, be sure to stop at the observation area located in the northeast corner of the National Wildlife Refuge (414-387-2658), near the intersection of Highway 49 and County Z.

Although you can bicycle the parkway, a better option for cyclists is the 34-mile Wild Goose State Trail. Connecting Fond du Lac and the tiny crossroads of Clyman Junction via an abandoned railroad corridor, the trail, which is closed to motorized traffic in the fall, hugs the western edge of the marsh. It's a popular hiking route as well.

By its very nature, the marsh itself affords limited opportunities for hiking. Three trails, ranging from .4 to 2.5 miles in length, traverse the northwest corner of the refuge, while Quick's Point in the state wildlife area also offers several miles of scenic hiking. It's over these trails that DNR wildlife educator Bill Volkert leads most of his weekend naturalist programs, which cover such diverse topics as Horicon's Indian history, glacial geology (Horicon is one of the nine units that comprise Wisconsin's Ice Age National Scientific Reserve) and, yes, Canada geese. For information, call the DNR Horicon Office at (414) 387-7860. The nonprofit Marsh Haven Nature Center (414-386-2182), three miles east of Waupun on Highway 49, offers guided bus tours and a variety of education programs, and has its own system of hiking trails, a picnic area and an observation tower.

Still, there is only one way to get to the heart of Horicon: the water. While the northern two-thirds of the marsh (the federal portion) is closed to all boating, the state-managed southern third abounds with opportunities for canoeing. Greenhead Landing, on the east branch of the Rock River, is the favored put-in. Blue Heron Landing (414-485-4663; 485-2942), in downtown Horicon, offers canoe rentals, shuttle service and pontoon boat tours of the marsh.

IN THE AREA

At the risk of mixing metaphors, when the geese return to Horicon, the cities surrounding the marsh put on the dog. Waupun holds a German Volksfest in September,

and in October Mayville celebrates Audubon Days while Horicon showcases Art on the Marsh. (See sidebar for details.)

As for other attractions, the Galloway House and Village, open through September (336 E. Pioneer Rd.; 414-922-6390), includes a 30-room restored Victorian home, general store, schoolhouse, toy shop, grist mill and photo studio. At Larson's Famous Clydesdales, 20 miles west of Fond du Lac (414-748-5466), you can meet the giant horses face to face and watch them go through their steps in full harness. In Waupun, check out the monumental bronzes in the city park, notably James Earl Fraser's "End of the Trail," for which Waupun has earned the title "City of Sculpture." To capture the flavor of the season, nip up the east shore of Lake Winnebago on Highway 151 to the Little Farmer Orchard, where you can sample freshly pressed cider, dip your own caramel apples, or take a hayride to the pumpkin patch. ■

WINTER *escapes*

Shimmering snow, crackling air,

radiant blue skies—winter is

no time for hibernating!

Bundle up the kids for a sleigh ride

through the frosty countryside.

Herald the season at a

holiday festival. Experience

the magic of a candlelight ski.

With music, bonfires,

fireworks, parades,

Wisconsin winter means fun.

1 CROSS-COUNTRY SKIING

AMERICA'S BIGGEST SKI RACE

They say cross-country skiing is the silent sport—uncrowded trails, serene forests—but many willingly give up the usual atmosphere to partake in one great event: the American Birkebeiner. The 52-kilometer race is modeled after the Norwegian Birkebeiner, which itself commemorates the rescue, in 1206, of Norway's infant king by two Viking skiers.

The American "Birkie" begins at Telemark Resort near Cable and traverses a hilly, wooded course to downtown

Skiers take off at the American Birkebeiner.

Hayward. Despite being considered the most grueling ski marathon in the world, 6,000 skiers participate. If you're not up for doing the whole distance, a companion race, the Kortelopet, ends at the 25-kilometer mark. The American Birkebeiner takes place in late February. For more information, call (715) 634-5025.

2 FESTIVAL

A HOT AIR AFFAIR

Without a doubt, "Moon Glow"—a nighttime spectacle of some 40 hot air balloons—is the most captivating event of Hudson's Hot Air Affair. But there's lots more to enjoy at this winter festival, held the last weekend in February.

Want offbeat fun? You'll find it at Friday evening's downtown "torchlight parade." The torchlight comes from the hot-air balloon burners, which illuminate a parade of decorated balloon baskets. Marching bands of kazoo players ("Kazoos don't freeze to your lips!" point out parade officials) provide entertainment, as they vie for the winning musical routine.

On Saturday there is zaniness: snow volleyball, skijoring and smoosh boarding. In the latter event, two- and four-member teams bound through the snow, as best they can, with two-by-fours strapped to

their feet. For the musically inclined, there are dances at Dick's Bar & Grill and other festival locales all weekend. And for those seeking beauty? Take in the colorful sky at the 7:30 a.m. balloon launches Saturday and Sunday and the 3 p.m. balloon launch on

Balloons ready for lift-off in Hudson.

Saturday. Or follow the candlelit cross-country ski trails Friday night at Willow River State Park. Call (715) 386-8411.

3 CROSS-COUNTRY SKIING

LEARN AND ENJOY

If all you want to do is ski, you can slap on a pair of boards and tromp around anyplace there's snow on the ground. But if you'd like to fall in love with the sport, then go to Trees for Tomorrow in Eagle River. Instructors here teach you not only how to stride and glide, but help you understand the glorious wintry world to which skiing gives you access.

Trees for Tomorrow, a non-

Get close to nature at Trees for Tomorrow.

profit organization that operates in cooperation with the U.S. Forest Service, offers weekend ski packages that include lodging, meals and, if desired, ski instruction. Equipment may be rented. Guests stay in dormitories with private bedrooms and shared bathrooms. Children are welcome.

One of the best features of Trees for Tomorrow is its location—near more than 100 kilometers of ski trails that wind through Nicolet and Northern Highland-American Legion forests. Another is the

center's nature program. Six resident naturalists talk in depth on such subjects as wolves, bats or the winter stars. For more information, call (715) 479-6456.

4 FESTIVAL

NORTHERN EXPOSURE

Organizers of Shawano's Northern Exposure winter festival are quick to point out that they thought up the catchy title all by themselves, and the fact that it was also the name of a former TV show is pure coincidence. There are, however, some resemblances between "Northern Exposure" (the TV show) and Northern Exposure (the event): namely, animals, craziness, romance.

The TV show had moose, Shawano is overrun with dogs—sled dogs that race in the festival's companion event, the Wolf River Rendezvous. Sanctioned by the International Sled-Dog Racing Association, the race draws 75 teams from Europe, Canada and the U.S. Free dog-sled rides are offered for the kids.

As for craziness, there is ice-fishing. Anglers in Northern Exposure's tournament catch walleye, northern and perch. Also in the craziness category is the snowshoe race, which draws "just ordinary"—in other words, clumsy—people, according to the chamber of commerce.

And in Shawano, romance means a candlelight ski (weather permitting), horse-drawn carriage rides and a Saturday night dance. Events are held at Shawano County Park and the Shawano Lake Golf Club. The festival usually occurs in mid-January; for more information call (800) 235-8528.

5 PERFORMANCE

A NUTCRACKER TO REMEMBER

The enchanting dance of the Sugar Plum Fairy. Clara's magical sleigh ride through the winter night sky. The fearsome battle between the Nutcracker and the Evil Rat King. There are countless classic moments in "The Nutcracker" ballet, and they unfold like holiday ribbon in thousands of stage productions across America each winter. But there is something so captivating about the Central Wisconsin School of Ballet's performance in Wausau that it has received national attention. What could it be?

The mice. "Their little faces show under the fake snouts," *Newsweek* magazine declared in a short list of the country's "Notable Nutcrackers." And the dancers. Sixty perform, and not all are students of ballet. In past years, the first act has featured a doctor, a minister, a dentist and other community members. Guest

performers include dancers from the Milwaukee Ballet. And the stage is a fine one: Wausau's Grand Theater. This Classical-Revival structure was built in 1927 and has undergone a $2 million restoration, resulting in a truly exquisite sound system. The perfomance usually occurs in early December; for tickets, call (715) 842-4447.

Central Wisconsin School of Ballet's "The Nutcracker."

6 EVENT

CATCH THE SPIRIT AT HERITAGE HILL

Walk through the gate at Heritage Hill, the state park that slopes down to the Fox River in Green Bay, and you step back in time, back through the history that shaped northeastern Wisconsin. There's the garrulous French fur trader, puffing on his clay pipe, bartering his beads and trinkets; there's the blunt-spoken blacksmith, forging a new set of shoes

Sharing a Christmas story at Heritage Hill.

for the banker's saddle horse; and there's the earnest Belgian farmer, milking his cows.

Heritage Hill is a living museum, and never more so than during its Spirit of Christmas Past celebration, a two-week event that usually begins the second weekend in November. No chain-clanking, bony-fingered Marleys here. Each building is decorated in a manner appropriate to its era and ethnic tradition, and interpreters, costumed in Christmas finery, spread the Yuletide joy. At the 1871 Beaupre House, for example, interpreters re-create formal holiday teas and dinners; at the 1901 Belgian farmstead, a "family" eagerly anticipates the arrival of St. Nicholas.

Heritage Hill, open daily during this two-week period, is located at 2640 S. Webster Ave., in Green Bay. For more information call (414) 448-5150.

7 EVENT
ARTFUL MERRIMAKING

Green Bay's Arti Gras has got to be one of the biggest entertainment bargains of the season. For a few dollars, you can view or buy the work of 90 artists at a juried show and sale, visit with Green Bay Packers players and get their autographs, be entertained by singers and magicians, and go for a horse and carriage ride. You can even have your fortune told—a fitting activity for the first month of the new year. Drop the kids off at the children's tent, and volunteers will keep the little ones entertained while you attend to such weighty matters.

Arti Gras, a benefit for the scholarship fund of the Northeastern Wisconsin Arts Council, is held in late January at the Brown County Expo Center. Call (414) 494-9507 for exact dates.

8 TRAIN RIDE
DASHING THROUGH SNOW WITH SANTA

St. Nick's aboard, and you should be too, when the Santa Claus Express leaves the Mid-Continent Railway Depot in North Freedom for a delightful eight-mile chug through the countryside. During a late-November weekend, the turn-of-the-century steam engine will blow its whistle at 10 a.m. sharp to announce the first of the day's several departures. Santa will hand out small gift bags for the kids, while doing his best to memorize their exhaustive Christmas lists. And if Mom and Dad want to give themselves an early present, they can spring for first-class tickets, which include beverage and hors d'oeuvres. Or take the Sunday afternoon brunch train, and enjoy a lavish, five-course dinner. Call (608) 522-4261 for more information.

9 EVENT

HIGH-FLYING SKIERS

Ski-jumping may not be our most popular sport, but it surely is the most spectacular. Years ago, Wisconsin had jumps throughout the state, most built by Scandinavian immigrants with a passion for skiing and a desire to fly. Wisconsin is still a center for jumping, home to five jumps. The second weekend in February, you can watch the action at the Intercontinental Cup Ski-Jumping Tournament, one in a series of international competitions, held near Westby. The tournament draws athletes from all over the world, and features two jumps: a 112K slope, one of the biggest in the U.S., for the main event and a smaller hill for a junior competition.

The Snowflake ski-jump grounds are on County P between Westby and Coon Valley. Food and refreshments are available, and tailgating is encouraged. For more information, call (608) 634-3211.

10 NATURE

EAGLES ON VIEW

Until the 1800s, bald eagles bred throughout Wisconsin, but as our state was settled their numbers drastically diminished. By 1950, eagles were no longer found in the southern two-thirds of the

Intercontinental Cup Ski-Jumping Tournament near Westby.

Bald eagle near Cassville.

state, victims of hunting, habitat destruction and pesticides. Eventually, even populations in the far north plummeted.

But like a grand Hollywood star, the bald eagle has made a comeback. Thanks to state recovery efforts, there have been more than 400 breeding pairs of eagles in Wisconsin in recent years, up from 82 pairs in 1970.

Most of our eagles spend the summer up north, breeding and raising their young. But in the winter many move to southern Wisconsin, especially to areas along rivers where a dam has created a pool of open water in which the birds can swoop down for fish. A number of these areas are located along the Mississippi River near Cassville. And here, in late January, organizers will help you view and learn about our magnificent national emblem.

Observation sites at Riverside Park and Nelson Dewey State Park are staffed by knowledgeable volunteers, and spotting scopes are available for close-up views. Guided bus trips take riders into the countryside, where eagles can be seen feeding on carrion in the fields. Programs on the bald eagle and other birds of prey are presented in the high school gym. And, when your eyes have gotten their fill of eagles, you can take a hayride through Stonefield Historic Site or walk by candlelight

through Nelson Dewey State Park. Call (608) 725-5855 for exact dates.

11 FESTIVAL

A VERY TRADITIONAL HOLIDAY

New Year's Eve at Folklore Village in Dodgeville is marked by an Old World celebration, a night of feasting and dancing that culminates under the winter sky at midnight. As the clock strikes 12, a bonfire of 50 Christmas trees sends flames 30 feet high, and the singing of guests echoes across the snowy countryside.

The New Year's Eve celebration is the culmination of Folklore Village's five-day Festival of Christmas and Mid-Winter Traditions, which includes traditional meals, afternoon teas, dance and folk art sessions, an evening party and a children's program. To participate on New Year's Eve, you must be registered for other festival events. For reservations, call (608) 924-4000 by December 1.

12 FESTIVAL

CELEBRATING SWISS-STYLE

Bathed in the warm light of a bonfire, yodelers and alphorn players send a song of Switzerland over the hills of southern Wisconsin. Some, dressed in Swiss costume, might seem out of place and time. But this is New Glarus, also known as "Little Switzerland," and this night they are celebrating the passing of winter.

Friday night's bonfire is just one of many traditional events planned for the February Winterfest in this Green County village. A bluegrass festival and fiddle contest, a cross-country ski race and a Winterfest Parade round out the weekend.

Those who come inside from the cold will find wood-carving and art, quilt and collectibles shows in the high school. The fest also features a guided hike on the Ice Age Trail and the Winterfest Dance at the New Glarus Hotel. And don't miss the sleigh rides, hayrides, snowmobiling and cross-country skiing, which occur all weekend long. Call (608) 527-2095 for details.

13 EVENT

SWIMMING WITH BEARS—BRRR!

An unsuspecting passerby near Sheboygan's Municipal Armory on New Year's morning just might do a double take. With primal sounds of hooting, chanting and stomping emanating from the brick edifice, and the almost exotic smell of bratwurst drifting from its seams, one might wonder if some secret society was practic-

ing an ancient rite of passage. And, in a sense, one would be correct.

This is the day the Sheboygan "Polar Bears" hit the beach, the ice and the slushy waves of Lake Michigan as they have for more than 25 years. Why? "Because it's there!" they'll tell you.

Members acknowledge that so-called Polar Bears do the same crazy thing in Menasha, Milwaukee, even Chicago, but the comparison is like turkey dogs to brats: in sheer numbers, scope and character, Sheboygan's got the beef. The veteran Polar Bears are dressed in the most outlandish costumes—sea monsters, cave people, diaper-clad New Year's

Polar Bear swimmers hit the surf near Sheboygan.

babies, and the ever popular ensemble of cut-offs and a crash helmet. After a pre-plunge party at the Armory, nearly 400 thick-skinned thrill seekers join them in the water, and several thousand other folks cheer them on. Within a minute or two, most folks make a hasty retreat, clawing their way up the snowbanks at the shoreline. Once in a while you'll see some true swimmers practicing their breast stroke, but with the water temperature averaging 35 degrees and wind-chill averaging minus 23, nobody stays in for long.

The post-plunge party at the Armory, however, goes on till well after every goosebump has faded and every brat has

Bolz Conservatory at Olbrich Gardens in Madison.

hit the grill. The Armory is located on 516 Broughton Drive. For more information, call (414) 457-9495.

14 NATURE

ESCAPE TO THE TROPICS

Even those who enjoy winter occasionally find themselves weary of the cold and snow. The perfect remedy is a visit to a warm, steamy rain forest.

Two conservatories, Mitchell Park Domes in Milwaukee and Olbrich Gardens in Madison, provide miraculous retreats from winter weariness. Both offer a paradise under glass where you can stroll down pathways through lush tropical plantlife, pause on bridges over pools, and sit on benches by a waterfall. Short of buying a plane ticket to the tropics, it's as far away from winter as you can get. At Milwaukee's conservatory, you can continue into a second dome featuring a desert environment, then into a third that is filled with rotating seasonal displays. Olbrich Gardens also sets up a special display for the holiday season.

Mitchell Park Domes is located at 524 S. Layton Blvd. in Milwaukee; call (414) 649-9800 for hours. Olbrich Botanical Gardens is located at 3330 Atwood Ave. in Madison; call (608) 246-4551 for hours.

15 ARTS

SNOW ART

In January, teams of artists from around the world descend on Milwaukee to carve, chisel and mold the most transient of all mediums—snow—into large-scale works of art. In the U.S. International Snow Sculpting Competition, each team starts with a 6-by-6-by-10-foot block of snow, which it works on for four days. Then the public votes for the winner of the People's Choice Award. The artists themselves cast votes in a formal judging of creativity, technique and message. The competition is held outside the Marcus Center for the Performing Arts. Call (414) 273-7121 for dates.

Snow sculpting competition in Milwaukee.

16 MUSEUM

TOPS IN TOPS

When producers at Hollywood's Metro-Goldwyn-Mayer Studios (MGM) began work on a movie called *My Summer Story*, they realized they'd need to call in an expert on spinning tops, an integral part of the plot. Enter Judith Schultz, owner of the Spinning Top Exploratory Museum in Burlington. Serving as technical advisor and teaching cast members to throw, the "top lady," as she came to be known on the set, had the time of her life.

Her Hollywood days are over now, but back in Wisconsin the spin doctor continues to spread her enthusiasm—an enthusiasm backed by a collection of 2,000 tops, yo-yos, gyroscopes and other toys. Visit the Spinning Top Exploratory Museum and you'll do more than gaze into display cases: Schultz will personally guide you through a 90-minute program of videos, tricks, games and challenges. "It's very hands-on," she says. "And I try to sprinkle it with tidbits of history and science." If you decide to go, be sure to call first, as Shultz's tours are given at specified times only. Call (414) 763-3946.

17 EVENT

A FEAST FIT FOR A KING

Lords and ladies, pages and wenches, nobles and peasants: All mingle freely in the richly textured pageant that is Kenosha's Ye Olde Englishe Christmasse Feaste. It's like going back 400 years to a mead hall in merry old England, with magical nonstop entertainment—everything from madrigal singers, Scottish bagpipers and Shakespearean actors to jesters, jugglers and tumblers.

And the food is fit for kings and queens. The nine-course Falstaffian banquet begins with hot wassail, moves on to beef barley soup and salad greens, then settles down to smoked trout, Cornish game hens and pork roast, complemented by candied sweet yams and green beans almondine. This sturdy fair is served family style on enormous platters. After an intermezzo of fruits and cheeses, the piece de resistance appears: a spectacular flamed plum pudding.

The affair is held in December at St. Mark's Alstadt auditorium. To purchase tickets, call (414) 942-2230.

18 CROSS-COUNTRY SKIING

STRIDING BY CANDLELIGHT

For a memorable evening, schuss through a silent forest illuminated only by candle or torch. Candlelight skis are suitable for even beginning skiers since gentle, easy trails are used. Some parks provide bonfires and lit cooking grills.

The following is a list of parks that usually hold candlelight skis, but please call for verification.

Lake Kegonsa State Park
Stoughton, (608) 873-9695
Black River State Forest
Black River Falls, (715) 284-1400
Wildcat Mountain State Park
Ontario, (608) 337-4775
Blue Mound State Park
Blue Mounds, (608) 437-5711
Lake Wissota State Park
Chippewa Falls, (715) 382-4574
Perrot State Park
La Crosse, (608) 534-6409
Torchlite Tour and Bonfire Ski
Crivitz, (715) 854-3231
Kettle Moraine State Forest
Delafield, (414) 646-3025
Interstate Park
St. Croix Falls, (715) 483-3747
Newport State Park
Ellison Bay, (414) 854-2500
Mirror Lake State Park
Baraboo, (608) 254-2333
Council Grounds State Park
Merrill, (715) 536-4502
Merrick State Park
Fountain City, (608) 687-4136
Governor Dodge State Park
Dodgeville, (608) 935-2315
Red Cedar Trail
Menomonie, (715) 232-2652
Willow River State Park
Hudson, (715) 386-5931
Bong State Recreation Area
Kansasville, (414) 878-5600
Kettle Moraine State Forest
Campbellsport, (414) 626-2116
High Cliff State Park
Menasha, (414) 989-1106
Kohler-Andrae State Park
Sheboygan, (414) 451-4080
Wyalusing State Park
Bagley, (608) 996-2261
Pike Lake State Park
Hartford, (414) 644-5248
Hartman Creek State Park
Waupaca, (715) 258-2372

weekend **ADVENTURES**

Enjoy Christmas shopping at its best—in Cedarburg, a village that is as rich in history as it is in goods. Discover holiday magic in Sturgeon Bay's garlanded storefronts, hayrides and teas. And relish winter as it was meant to be, up in the snowy North Woods.

BAYFIELD
CABLE
HAYWARD
MINOCQUA
EAGLE RIVER
STURGEON BAY
CEDARBURG

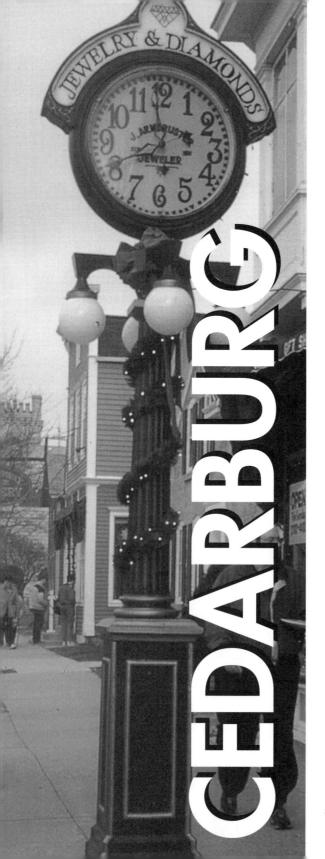

CEDARBURG

Shopping Through Cedarburg

L ike many Wisconsin
towns, Cedarburg
began with a mill. In
the mid-19th century, German
immigrants Friederich Hilgen
and Walter Schroeder cleared a
road into the frontier north of
Milwaukee, built a grist mill
alongside the rushing Cedar
Creek, and solicited settlers.
Settlers came—mostly fellow
Germans, who crafted sturdy,
distinctive buildings of local
limestone. These buildings
served the people of Cedarburg
well, until the 1960s, that is,
when developers, under the
banner of "modernization,"
began to tear them down.
Luckily, a few diligent individ-
uals decided to buck the trend.
One couple bought the huge
woolen mill at the end of town
and created a winery. Someone
else led the fight to save handsome St. Francis Borgia
Church. Over the course of a

*Washington Avenue, bedecked for
the holidays.*

decade, preservationists scraped, painted and patched the buff-colored buildings flanking main street, then transformed them into picturesque, and highly successful, specialty shops, inns and restaurants.

Today, downtown Cedarburg contains 104 buildings on the National Register of Historic Places. With a downtown that looks almost as it did a century ago, the city is a Christmas wonderland, its main street bedecked in lights and garland like an exquisite holiday gift.

CHRISTMAS IN THE COUNTRY

An average of 30,000 people a month visit Cedarburg, lured by its quaint buildings, unique wares and the special events organized to highlight the town's charms. On the first weekend in December, the big draw is Christmas in the Country, a juried arts and crafts show featuring some of the loveliest, best-executed items around, most Wisconsin made.

Four friends—Sandra Pape, Luella Doss, Susan Hale and Betty Schmidt—founded Christmas in the Country more than 20 years ago as an outlet for their own artistry. Today 75 artists, primarily women, exhibit their work here. Held in the giant woolen-mill-turned-winery, the show

specializes in high-quality, unique crafts—at least one-third of each artist's inventory must be made especially for this event.

Ozaukee County Pioneer Village.

The variety of items for sale is extraordinary. In recent years you could buy richly colored redware, all-natural wreaths, hooked rugs, whimsical dolls and wrought-iron lamps, along with Christmas ornaments, decoupage clocks, carved wooden Santas, herbed vinegars and playful quilted jackets

Ozaukee County Pioneer Village.

that quality draws crowds, and Christmas in the Country is no exception. When you pay admission, you are given a ticket with a number, and ticket-holders are allowed into the show in waves based on those numbers. This method assures a comfortable shopping experience, but you should be prepared for a wait—up to three hours—if you arrive at the busiest times.

The show is open Thursday through Sunday. Organizers say the least-crowded periods are Thursday and Friday afternoons, and Friday evening. If you do face a wait, don't fret. Shoppers need not stand in line, though the free spiced tea and home-baked cookies offered there are delicious. Use your waiting period instead to tour the rest of Cedarburg, which is quite a treat itself.

embellished with felt Christmas trees. The four organizers display their own work as well. Pape creates jewelry of handmade paper and metallic paint; Veronica Hammes (who replaced Betty Schmidt in 1981) concentrates on wearable art; Hale, whose work is collected worldwide, makes dolls; Luella Doss, who now designs for Simplicity Pattern Company, crafts big, fanciful stuffed chickens—the kind of item that sounds crazy but is so delightful and skillfully done you can't help but want to bring a whole flock home.

Be forewarned, however,

THE CITY

Cedarburg's downtown stretches a mere six blocks along Washington Avenue, just the right distance for leisurely shopping and historic exploration. The Chamber of Commerce's walking tour booklet, "A Walk Through Yesterday in Cedarburg, Wisconsin" (available at the Cedarburg Visitor Center and Washington House Inn, both on Washington Avenue), will guide you around.

Start with a ramble through the Cedar Creek Settlement,

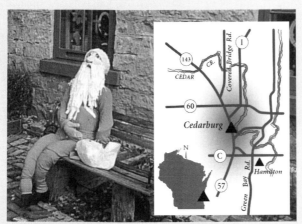

Share a bench with Santa at Christmas in the Country.

EATING WELL

Roma's Deli—One of Cedarburg's best-kept secrets, this informal place, with four formica tables, tends to be refreshingly uncrowded. Order a sweet and tasty barbequed-pork sandwich at the counter. W62 N603 Washington Ave. (414) 375-4321.

T.J. Ryan's—This friendly tavern assembles sandwiches to your order. Try the pungent liverwurst between thick slices of dark rye. W62 N599 Washington Ave. (414) 376-0007.

Settlers Inn—Joan and Tom Dorsey's menu includes a delicious German sausage platter, grilled sandwiches and thick cheese soup, served in a smoke-free environment. Since Joan is a registered dietician, about one-third of the menu is low-fat. W63 N657 Washington Ave. (414) 377-4466.

Barth's on the Bridge—A traditional favorite, Barth's serves baked meatloaf, roast duck, hot and cold sandwiches, and a yummy navy bean soup, among other dishes. N 58 W6194 Columbia Rd. (414) 377-0660.

Victor's—A gourmet menu features julienne of veal frangelico (veal sauteed with mushrooms and hazelnut cream, served on poppy-seed pasta) and a luscious caramel-chocolate-cashew cheesecake. W62 N547 Washington Ave. (414) 375-1777.

Beernsten's Candy—When energy levels drop, stop here for hand-dipped chocolates, fudge and candy canes. A sampler bag of chocolates costs $1. Located in the Stagecoach Inn, W61 N520 Washington Ave. (414) 377-9512.

LODGING

Washington House Inn—Elegant accommodations in an 1886 Cream City brick building feature Victorian furnishings, fireplaces and whirlpool baths. (800) 554-4717.

Stagecoach Inn Bed & Breakfast—This 1855 Greek Revival stone building has been splendidly restored and comfortably furnished with antiques and private baths. (414) 375-0208.

Port Washington Inn Bed & Breakfast—About 10 miles northeast of Cedarburg, the Port Washington Inn offers four-poster beds, lace-trimmed quilts and other creature comforts in a Victorian setting. (414) 284-5583.

American Country Farm—An 1844 restored landmark stone cottage, a few miles south of Cedarburg in Mequon. (414) 242-0194.

WINTER EVENTS

Christmas in the Country—This annual art show is held Thursday through Sunday the first weekend in December. On Friday through Sunday of the same weekend, the Cedarburg Community Center hosts their arts and crafts fair, "That Christmas Feeling"; the Cedarburg Cultural Center sponsors the "Festival of Trees," during which you can bid on decorated trees and wreaths; and the Christmas House, a decorated Victorian home, is open for tours. The Ozaukee County Pioneer Museum presents its Christmas event, featuring hands-on activities for children, Saturday and Sunday.

Winter Festival—One of Wisconsin's oldest winter festivals, this event features family skating, bed races on the frozen pond, an ice-carving contest and a sock hop. Held the first weekend in February.

IN OTHER SEASONS

A Day in the Country Folk Art Show—Arts and crafts by 50 Midwest folk artists are displayed. Held in April.

Stone and Century House Tour—A self-guided tour of several century-old homes. Held in June.

Strawberry Festival—Live entertainment, arts and crafts, hayrides, a pig roast and, of course, lots of strawberries. Held in June.

Wine and Harvest Festival—Celebrate the harvest with a grape-stomping contest, scarecrow building and a farmers' market, among other activities. Held the third weekend in September.

Maxwell Street Days—You can buy almost anything at this flea market, held four times a year.

For more information, contact the Cedarburg Chamber of Commerce, (414) 377-9620.

Covered Bridge Park.

THE LAST COVERED BRIDGE IN WISCONSIN

Years ago, more than 40 covered bridges crossed Wisconsin streams. Today, only one remains: the Cedar Creek Bridge. Originally called the "Red Bridge," it is now a weathered grey, and spans Cedar Creek north of Cedarburg.

The bridge was built in 1876 after neighboring farmers petitioned the town of Cedarburg to replace an existing bridge that was subject to wash-outs whenever the creek flooded. Pine logs were cut and milled near Baraboo, then hauled to the site where they were fitted and set in place. Interlacing 3-by-10-inch planks were secured with 2-inch hardwood pins, a method that eliminated the use of nails or bolts. This construction is known as "lattice truss," and is now very rare. As with all covered bridges, the roof and a board-and-batten exterior protected the timbers.

After 85 years of continuous service, the bridge was placed in semi-retirement; a modern span was built alongside it to accommodate two lanes of automobile traffic. You can, however, still walk across the old covered bridge. When you do, make sure to admire its beautiful form, and listen to the echo of your footsteps on the sturdy wooden planks.

Covered Bridge Park is located on Covered Bridge Road, near the intersection of Highway 143 and Highway 60, north of Cedarburg. The park, a pleasant spot along Cedar Creek, has picnic tables, grills, restrooms and drinking water.

the old mill at the north end of Washington Avenue where Christmas in the Country is held. Among a number of different stores there, the Accent Shop features a huge collection of ribbons, dried flowers, pine cones, grape vines and other materials for crafting holiday decorations. Farther down Washington Avenue, the 1870 August Weber Residence houses Gifts from the Old Country, where you can purchase German Christmas tree ornaments, Austrian lace and Russian nesting dolls. The Cedarburg Cheesary, in the same building, sells various cheeses cut to order and Swedish lingonberry jam.

Keep on strolling and you'll come to (among other neat shops) Ye Old Stencil House, in the 1870 Greco-Italianate John Roth Residence, featuring more stencil patterns than one could ever imagine; Stornoway House Gallery, with gleaming oak furniture and beautiful watercolors by regional artists; and the Nouveau Antique and Goldsmith Parlor, one of Cedarburg's most striking buildings, painted violet with purple trim. Formerly a blacksmith shop, the store sells lovely antique jewelry and china dolls.

Even if you're not in the mood for shopping, there's plenty to look at. Coast to Coast Hardware, for example, is housed in an imposing, three-story Italianate structure; Landmark Supply Company does business in the massive, five-story grist mill built by Cedarburg founders Hilgen and Schroeder, now considered one of the finest mills in the Midwest. And on Christmas in the Country weekend, the Cedarburg Cultural Center gives tours of the 1849 Kuhefuss House. One of the oldest residences in Cedarburg, the building offers a fascinating glimpse of what life was like in a German-American household. All told, you'll find you can easily spend an afternoon wandering up and down Washington Avenue, admiring arched windows, gracious porches, cast-iron ornamentation and the other marks of skilled craftsmanship that Cedarburg proves can well stand the test of time.

Trolleys transport carolers and visitors.

IN THE AREA

For the most part, Cedarburg is a place for grown-ups, so if you have children along, consider taking a side trip to the Ozaukee County Pioneer Village, a living museum about 10 miles north of town on Highway I. Here, a collection of 17 buildings dates from 1840 to 1907. Generally open only from Memorial Day through mid-October, the museum hosts a special Christmas event designed to teach children about holiday traditions from days gone by. Children may make potato stencils, paper puppets and button toys, or sing Christmas carols accompanied by an old pump organ. There's also an old-fashioned store stocked with the kind of small, inexpensive toys and candies that kids love. For other interesting side trips head to Covered Bridge Park (on Covered Bridge Road north of Cedarburg), where you can walk across the last remaining covered bridge in Wisconsin, and historic Hamilton (one mile southeast of downtown Cedarburg), an 1840s community with a beautiful collection of stone homes, outbuildings and mill. ∎

STURGEON BAY

A Sturgeon Bay Holiday

According to conventional wisdom, there are really three Door Counties. The best-known is Northern Door, the Door County of precipitous limestone bluffs, sparkling sand beaches, spectacular sunsets, goats on the roof and quaint shoreside villages brimming with vacationers. The least-known is Southern Door, a pastoral landscape of cherry orchards, dairy farms and sturdy brick homesteads that testify to the region's status as America's premier outpost of rural Belgian culture and architecture. The third Door County, Sturgeon Bay, lies somewhere in the middle—geographically as well as in the popular imagination. It's a little like a circus rider, each foot on the back of a different horse.

Although tiny Baileys Harbor actually preceded it as the county seat, Sturgeon Bay has been the peninsula's commercial hub since the 1850s. Sawmills and stone quarries, the early cornerstones of the local economy, gave way to

Enjoy fine fare and holiday magic.

shipbuilding shortly after a canal was blasted along the historic Michigan-Sturgeon Bay portage in 1881. Nine years in construction, the 7,400-foot canal shaved a hundred miles from the Green Bay-Chicago water route. As many as 7,000 vessels traversed the canal in a single year during the height of the 19th-century lumber boom.

In recent years, the fortunes of Sturgeon Bay's famous shipbuilding industry have waned. The exception is Palmer Johnson, builder of luxury yachts. Although headquartered in Sturgeon Bay, PJs, as it's called, maintains offices in London, Tokyo, Dubai and the south of France.

These international connections notwithstanding, it would be a stretch to call this bisected-by-water city of 9,200 "cosmopolitan." Sturgeon Bay is, in most respects, no different than any other small Wisconsin municipality. It has its banks and auto dealerships, its bowling alleys and dart leagues, even its Wal-Mart. True, Sturgeon Bay is an uncommonly friendly place, and there is that elusive Door County cachet. But what conspicuously distinguishes the city is the wealth of beguiling inns, unique shops and festive seasonal events from which the traveler can pick and choose. They've helped transform Sturgeon Bay from

where you stop on your way up the peninsula into where you stop, period.

Inn at Cedar Crossing.

CHRISTMAS BY THE BAY

A good deal of Sturgeon Bay's quiet charm traces to its boasting two National Historic Districts. Primarily a residential area, the Louisiana/Seventh Avenue district features a number of impressive private homes of the late Queen Anne style, homes rendered even more enchanting by holiday decorations and the first soft snows. But the Third Avenue/Downtown historic district, especially Third Avenue itself, illuminated by graceful gaslight-style lamps and framed by nostalgic brick facades and inviting storefronts, is Sturgeon Bay's showpiece. (Pick up a free Sturgeon Bay guide at local businesses for a map.)

Downtown is also the focal point of Sturgeon Bay's holiday festivities, which begin on the

White Lace Inn.

third weekend in November with the Christmas Walk. After the lighting of the Christmas tree and come-one, come-all caroling Friday evening, Santa arrives in town Saturday morning for a parade in his honor down Third Avenue. Normally closed at this time of year, the Door County Historical Museum, at the corner of 4th and Michigan

(414-743-5809), welcomes visitors to its exhibits of pioneer and turn-of-the-century life on the peninsula. Sunday afternoon, Sturgeon Bay's inns and B&Bs, wreathed in holiday finery and exuding Christmas cheer, hold open house. Beginning at 2 p.m., the Inn at Cedar Crossing, 336 Louisiana St., serves its fabulous Christmas Tea, a buffet of sweets and savories "in proper British fashion," according to innkeeper Terry Wulf. Other Sunday afternoon events include free hayrides, free movies for the children at the Donna Theater (239 N. Third Ave., 414-743-3569), a Christmas Craft Fair at the Bay Shore Inn (a mile north of the city on Bay Shore Drive) and a Country Folk Art Fair at the Sturgeon Bay YMCA (117 S. 5th St., 414-743-4949), with all proceeds benefiting the Y's Partners With Youth program.

Of course, you'll want to do some holiday shopping along the way. Several of Sturgeon Bay's more intriguing merchants hold forth on Jefferson Street, the main feeder into Third Avenue. Here Gold & Silver Creations offers exquisite handcrafted jewelry, while Everlastings specializes in imaginative dried and silk flower arrangements. A couple doors down, Cornucopia is a mecca for cooks and lovers of gourmet foods. Jefferson Street Antiques features, among other

EATING WELL

The Inn at Cedar Crossing—
Acclaimed for its consistently innovative cuisine, the inn serves breakfast, lunch and dinner year-round. The chefs do wonderful things with veal, poultry and fresh seafood—although there are those who insist that the entrees are merely a preamble to the fabulous desserts. More casual fare can be had in the adjoining Pub. 336 Louisiana St. (414) 743-4249.

DalSanto's—Sharing the old train depot with the Cherryland Brewery, DalSanto's specializes in pasta, Italian-style sandwiches and other fare with a Mediterranean accent. 341½ N. Third Ave. (414) 743-6100.

Perry's Cherry Diner—This classic '50s-era malt shop, festooned with Elvis, Marilyn and James Dean memorabilia, features burgers, gyros, saucy waitresses and more. 230 Michigan St. (414) 743-9910.

Schartner's on the Shore—This is where in-the-know locals go for Friday night perch, Saturday night prime rib and perhaps a highball or two, all at reasonable prices. 4680 Bay Shore Dr. (414) 743-2421.

LODGING

The White Lace Inn—Actually three historic homes connected by a winding stone walkway, this "whimsical Victorian" inn doesn't merely pamper guests, it envelops them in comfort. (414) 743-1105.

The Scofield House Bed & Breakfast—Once the home of Sturgeon Bay's mayor, this ornate, turn-of-the-century Queen Anne offers six guest rooms filled with fine antiques, groaning-board breakfasts and the genteel aura of a bygone time. (414) 743-7727.

The Barbican Guest House—Here, the romance of a country inn blends with the privacy of a fine

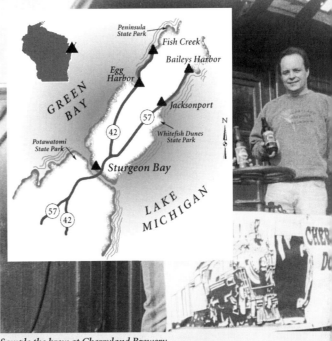

Sample the brew at Cherryland Brewery.

hotel. Eleven lavishly decorated two-room suites contain fireplaces, whirlpool baths, stereos, refrigerators and cable TVs. (414) 743-4854.

The Inn at Cedar Crossing—In the heart of Sturgeon Bay's downtown historic district, this impeccably restored century-old structure houses nine delightful guest rooms. The restaurant and pub are right downstairs. (414) 743-4200.

The Gray Goose Bed & Breakfast—Located a mile and a half north of town in a house that dates to the Civil War, this quiet, secluded B&B serves up full breakfasts and gracious hospitality at an affordable price. (414) 743-9100.

Maritime Inn—This centrally located Best Western motel sports an indoor pool and recreation area. (414) 743-7231; (800) 528-1234.

WINTER EVENTS

Christmas Walk—Downtown Sturgeon Bay hosts a parade, open

houses, craft fair, hayride and Christmas Tea. Held in November.

Christmas by Candlelight—Music, Christmas Tea, tours of Sturgeon Bay's inns and B&Bs with hayride transportation. Held in early December.

IN OTHER SEASONS

Taste of Door County—Sample the best dishes of more than 20 area restaurants. Held in July.

Door County Maritime Museum Festival—The area's maritime heritage is celebrated with boat exhibits, entertainment, a boat-building contest, boat tours, Coast Guard demonstrations and children's games. Held in August.

Harvest Fest—Art demonstrations, chili cook-off, music, farmers' market and hayrides, all on Third Avenue.

For more information, contact the Door County Chamber of Commerce, (414) 743-4456.

THE DOOR COUNTY FISH BOIL

The origins of the legendary Door County fish boil can't be precisely pinned down. But Scandinavians have been boiling fish for centuries, and it's believed that they brought the custom with them when they emigrated to the northern Door in the late-1800s. A good way to feed a lot of people with a minimum of fuss, the "boiled dinner" of fish (whitefish or lake trout), potatoes and onions soon caught on among the logging camps that then dotted the peninsula.

Later, Door County churches and civic groups began holding fish boils as fund-raising events. It was not until 1961 that the first commercial fish boil was offered at the Viking restaurant (now the Viking Grill) in Ellison Bay. Served with melted butter and wedges of lemon, and accompanied by coleslaw, rye bread and cherry pie, it proved such a hit that other restaurants quickly followed the Viking's lead. In short order, the humble but tasty Door County fish boil became one of the peninsula's most popular attractions.

The basic recipe has changed little in the past hundred years, except that whitefish is now used exclusively as lake trout is no longer a commercially fishable species in Lake Michigan. Diners sit outside and watch as their meal is being prepared: the salted water bubbling merrily, flames from the wood fire licking at the huge, blackened cauldron in which a wire mesh basket holding the ingredients is suspended. At the critical moment, the "master boiler" splashes a small measure of kerosene onto the fire, which results in a spectacular eruption of flame that causes the kettle to boil over. Yes, it's calculated to elicit "oohs" and "ahhs" from the audience, but it

Preparing a century-old recipe.

serves a culinary purpose, as well. The water that boils over carries with it oils and residues that would otherwise impart a strong, "fishy" flavor. A properly prepared boil is a delicious meal, the fish firm and sweet, the potatoes fork-tender but not mushy. Of course, the melted butter doesn't hurt anything—except your cholesterol level.

Any number of Door County restaurants offer fish boils in summer and fall, but the only place to enjoy one during the winter is the **White Gull Inn** in Fish Creek. Fish boils are served at the Gull on Wednesday and Saturday nights; reservations (414-868-3517) are a must.

items, furniture from the British Isles. Housed in a New England-style frame church built in 1881, Snowstar Ltd. has a dizzying array of cards, stationery, writing implements and what might be called "gifts for the literate."

After a strenuous bout of shopping, reward (and refresh) yourself by touring the Cherryland Brewery. Located on North Third Avenue in the old Ahnapee & Western train depot, this award-winning microbrewery is open seven days a week throughout the year. All of Cherryland's beers are hearty and flavorful, but be sure to sample Cherry Rail, a lively brew sweetened with a touch of cherry.

Sturgeon Bay's celebration of the season continues the first two weekends in December with Christmas by Candlelight. Up in Jacksonport (which the post office considers part of Sturgeon Bay), pianist-composer Dan Meunier plays traditional carols, as well as his own musical interpretations of Door County in winter Saturday afternoon from 2 to 4 p.m. at his intimate schoolhouse-studio. At 5 p.m., the Bay Shore Inn hosts a Christmas sing-along, complete with hot cider, cookies and a roaring fire. The Inn at Cedar Crossing reprises its Christmas Tea Sunday afternoon. Then, from 4 to 6 p.m., Sturgeon Bay's inns and B&Bs

afford a glimpse of Christmas past with twinkling white lights, fragrant garlands, whimsical decorations and their own special brand of heartfelt conviviality. Free hayrides whisk the mittened and muffled participants from inn to inn. Dickens himself would have applauded.

IN THE AREA

Some of the most enjoyable, family-friendly cross-country skiing in Wisconsin lies within striking distance of Sturgeon Bay. Peninsula Park, with its majestic Green Bay vistas and challenging network of trails, is only a half-hour drive north. Whitefish Dunes, with its own lofty view of Lake Michigan and excellent ski trails, is just 15 minutes from town. A third state park, Potawatomi, is virtually within a stone's throw of the city limits. Potawatomi not only offers an excellent system of cross-country trails (17 miles in all) but contains the only downhill ski area in Door County. Downhill and cross-country ski rentals are available at Mac's Sport Shop, 43 S. Madison Ave. (414-743-3350).

A popular attraction in the summertime, Cave Point (immediately north of Whitefish Dunes) is, if anything, even more spectacular in winter, when immense icicles hang from the wave-carved rock. Watch your footing on the ice-glazed stones. ■

NORTH WOODS

On Snow in the North Woods

Mounds of new-fallen snow as fluffy as pillows, air so crisp it crackles, the fresh smell of balsam fir. This is winter at its best—winter in Wisconsin's North Woods. To prosaic geographers, the North Woods is the area north of Highway 29. To the rest of us, it's where pine trees take over the landscape, where even blizzards are welcome, and where satisfaction is found in such simple pleasures as a snow-draped trail, a warm fire and a steaming cup of cocoa.

People have always been captivated by Wisconsin's northern tier. Lumbermen, of

Sixty inches of snow fall annually.

course, coveted its vast pine forest and took down the big trees around the turn of the century. Hunters and anglers followed, finding access to plentiful game and pristine lakes on the logging roads that sliced the countryside. By the 1920s, resorts lined the lakeshores, and rail cars chugged their way north full of vacationers in search of tranquillity.

Today, tourism is one of northern Wisconsin's major industries. Summer revolves around swimming and boating—Vilas County alone has the greatest concentration of inland lakes in the world. But in winter, the forest reigns. Sprung up on the ashes of the original North Woods, the sprawling conifer forest is crisscrossed with ski trails and snowmobile routes and dotted with downhill slopes. Best of all, with 60 inches of snow falling annually (more near Lake Superior), in winter it's almost always mantled in white.

You'll find opportunities for winter activities all across the north, but three regions serve as popular launching points: the Minocqua/Eagle River area, the Hayward/Cable area and the Bayfield Peninsula.

MINOCQUA/ EAGLE RIVER AREA

North Woods terrain is perfect for cross-country skiing: no big mountains, just lots of rolling hills and a variety of

landscapes to glide through, from spruce bogs and hemlock groves to stands of paper birch. The Minocqua/Eagle River area

Ski touring in the Nicolet National Forest.

is especially dense with nordic trails. Minocqua Winter Park (Squirrel Lake Road off Highway 70; 715-356-3309) west of Minocqua is the state's premier system, with 60 kilometers of manicured trails, a cozy chalet, a ski shop and ski school. Lessons are offered for

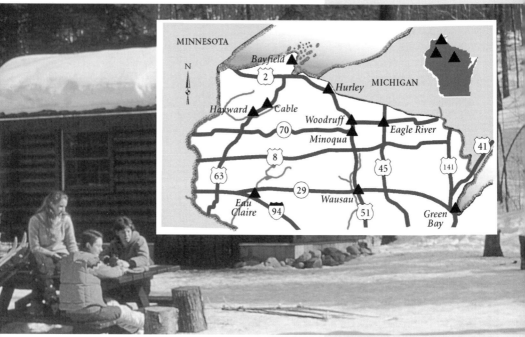

MINNESOTA

Bayfield

N

2

Hayward Cable

Hurley MICHIGAN

Woodruff

70

Minoqua

Eagle River

41

8

63

45

141

29

Eau
Claire 94

Wausau

51

Green
Bay

Taking a break along the Anvil Trail.

kids too, along with child care on weekends and holidays. The Nicolet National Forest east of Eagle River boasts a big system as well. You'll find a modern chalet and ski shop if you start out from the privately owned Eagle River Nordic (Butternut Lake Road, off Military Road; 715-479-7285). The Anvil Trail (off Highway 70; 715-479-2827) is outhouse only, but what is lost in amenities the scenery more than makes up for. Ski-skaters favor the undulating Razorback Ridges Ski Trails near Sayner (County N; 715-542-3019). Classical skiers relish Escanaba Lake (Nebish Lake Road, off Highway M north of Woodruff; 715-385-2727). Groomed for striding

EATING WELL

Jacobi's Hiawatha Inn—A fine gourmet restaurant located at the spot where the Hiawatha Special train once unloaded tourists. The garlic-stuffed tenderloin is a specialty. 9820 Cedar Falls Rd., Hazelhurst. (715) 356-5591.

Bosacki's Boat House—A family restaurant since 1917, Bosacki's is one of the North's best-known dining spots, with a menu that ranges from burgers to T-bone steaks. Highway 51, Minocqua. (715) 356-5292.

Ma Bailey's—The decor hearkens back to the years when this was a house of ill repute visited by Chicago mobsters. Nowadays duck, catfish and barbequed ribs attract the crowds. 8591 Woodruff Rd., Woodruff. (715) 356-6133.

The Guide's Inn—Elegant home-made fare, from the pate to the shrimp St. James, in a relaxed setting. County M, Boulder Junction. (715) 385-2233.

Chanticleer Inn—Enjoy prime rib and lobster tails in a dining room overlooking the chain of lakes. 1458 E. Dollar Lake Rd., Eagle River. (715) 479-4486.

Lost Land Lake Lodge—Crispy fried chicken and a Friday night fish fry reputed to be one of the best in the state. Even the tartar sauce is homemade. Brandt Road, off Highway 77 east of Hayward. (715) 462-3218.

Moose Cafe—Food from 4 a.m. Don't pass up the beef hash. Downtown Hayward. (715) 634-8449.

Old Rittenhouse Inn—Dinner here is not merely a meal but an event. Regional, seasonal specialties—fresh lake trout, locally raised lamb, wild mushrooms—are featured whenever possible, and desserts are spectacular. Reservations required. 301 Rittenhouse Ave. in Bayfield. (715) 779-5111.

Maggie's—The flamingos are fake but the food is real, with hearty, homemade soups, an astonishing variety of burgers and the best sauteed whitefish livers in Bayfield. 257 Manypenny. (715) 779-5641.

Greunke's First Street Inn—With tongue planted firmly in cheek, Greunke's embodies the nostalgic ambiance of a 1940s diner. This is where the wise gather for stacks of light-as-air pancakes. 17 N. First St. in Bayfield. (715) 779-5480.

LODGING

The Pointe Hotel and Conference Center—Luxurious one- and two-bedroom suites, indoor pool, whirlpool and sauna, near downtown Minocqua. (715) 356-4431.

Lakeview Motor Lodge—Comfortable units, in the thick of things in Minocqua. (715) 356-5208, (800) 852-1021.

Whip-Poor-Will Inn—A gorgeous modern log inn in Star Lake with sumptuous breakfasts. (715) 542-3600, (800) 788-5215.

Hintz's North Star Lodge—Lodge rooms with shared baths, apartments and villas, and good home cooking in the restaurant. Located in Star Lake. (715) 542-3600, (800) 788-5215.

Lumberman's Mansion Inn—The former home of North Wisconsin Lumber's general manager, this Hayward bed and breakfast features spacious rooms, neat old photos and soothing whirlpool baths. (715) 634-3012.

Spider Lake Lodge B&B—A rustic delight east of Hayward built in 1923 of tamarack logs. (800) OLD-WISC.

Ross' Teal Lake Lodge—A full-service resort in summer that exudes genuine old-time ambience, Ross' hunkers down in winter but keeps open a log cabin or two, along with modern suites. (715) 462-3631.

Telemark Resort—Two wings of rooms plus indoor pool, whirlpool, even indoor tennis courts and shops, east of Cable. (800) 472-3001.

Lakewoods Resort—A modern complex with the full array of motel amenities, east of Cable. (715) 794-2561.

Chanticleer Inn—Villas, cottages, townhouses, suites and rooms accommodate groups of all sizes, near Eagle River. (715) 479-4486, (800) 752-9193.

Old Rittenhouse Inn—The inn's 20 guest rooms, all with fireplaces and private baths, are located in three historic homes in Bayfield. (715) 779-5111.

Cooper Hill House—Comfortable lodging, private baths, in an 1888 home in Bayfield. (715) 779-5060.

Seagull Bay Motel—Low rates and a splendid view of Lake Superior, in Bayfield. (715) 779-5558.

Inn at Montreal—This former mining company office in Montreal is an informal bed and breakfast inn that welcomes families. (715) 561-5180.

WINTER EVENTS

Demo Days—Try the latest cross-country ski gear at Minocqua Winter Park in December.

World Championship Snowmobile Derby—Sled drivers from around the world compete in Eagle River in January.

Antique Snowmobile Derby—Sleds from the old days compete on the derby track. Held in Eagle River in February.

Klondike Days—Sled-dog races on the derby track, horse pull, log-splitting contest and a rendezvous. Held in Eagle River in February.

American Birkebeiner—Largest cross-country ski race in North America, Telemark to Hayward.

Winterfest—Snowmobile races, entertainment and dance. Held in Hayward in February.

IN OTHER SEASONS

Lumberjack World Championships—Chainsaw carving, log-rolling and other lumberjack contests. Held in Hayward in July.

Honor the Earth Powwow—Native American gathering, with drumming and dance. Held near Hayward in July.

Fat Tire Festival—Mountain-bike race, on the Birkie Trail near Hayward in September.

Cranberry Fest—Tours of the bogs, craft fair, walk/run and bike ride, and lots of cranberry treats. Held in Eagle River in October.

Bayfield Apple Festival—Food-stands galore, street entertainers, apple-peeling and pie-baking contests, capped off by a parade. Held the first weekend in October.

For more information, contact the Minocqua Chamber of Commerce, (800) 44-NORTH; Eagle River Information Bureau, (800) 359-6315; Hayward Area Chamber of Commerce, (800) 826-3474; Cable Area Chamber of Commerce, (800) 533-7454; Bayfield Chamber of Commerce, (715) 779-3335.

only, the narrow trails here pass through birch, hemlock and aspen woods, skirt three wilderness lakes, and practically cry out for you to go slow and smell the forest. Contact the Vilas County Advertising Department (715-479-3648) for a map showing 23 cross-country ski trails.

The North Woods is also snowmobile heaven. In fact, *Sno-Goer* magazine, a publication for snowmobile owners and organizations, names it the best snowmobile trail riding region in the country. The Minocqua/Eagle River area fairly roars with activity. If your heart races to the sound of a racing engine, be sure to catch the World Championship Snowmobile Derby (715-479-4424), held annually in Eagle River, where sleds reach speeds of a hundred miles an hour. The Snowmobile Racing Hall of Fame, in the derby headquarters, displays artifacts, photos and racing machines. If you lack your own vehicle, sign up for a tour of the area's groomed loops with Decker's Sno-Venture Tours (715-479-2764). The trips are guided and suitable for novices and families.

A free map of snowmobile trails throughout the state is available from the Wisconsin Division of Tourism, (800) 432-TRIP. Contact the Vilas County Advertising Department (715-479-3648) for their map showing the county's 550 miles of

Skiers at the start of the country's biggest ski race.

snowmobile trails. For additional maps of the region, call Oneida County, (715) 369-6140, and Forest County, (715) 478-2212.

HAYWARD/ CABLE AREA

Like a pale superhighway, the 30-foot-wide Birkie Trail traverses the Chequamegon National Forest from Telemark Resort to Hayward. This is the scene of the biggest cross-country ski event in North America—the marathon-length American Birkebeiner race (800-722-3386). On one weekend in February, the world's best skiers converge here, along with 6,000 others who want to test their mettle. Pasta suppers and other festivities abound, but lodging is at a premium so make reservations early if you want to be part of the hoopla. If you simply want to try out the trail, come another time— the Birkie Trail is free and open to the public whenever sufficient snow is on the ground. Access is from Highway OO southeast of Hayward or from Telemark Resort.

Telemark Resort itself (County M east of Cable; 715-798-3811) is the granddaddy of Wisconsin's nordic centers—its sinuous World Cup Trail was built for the World Cup nordic ski races. There's also a family-friendly downhill slope, a chalet conveniently located at its foot and a kids ski program. Adding

to the convenience: The resort includes condominiums and a large motel with a swimming pool and whirlpool.

Cross-country skiers should explore the Rock Lake trails, a short jog east of Telemark on County M. Tucked into the Chequamegon National Forest, enhanced by neither a shelter nor indoor plumbing, this system can seem like the middle of nowhere. But that's precisely

Snowmobile race at Hayward's Winterfest.

its charm. Take the long, isolated 16-kilometer loop and wind through big timber where heavy snows bend tree branches almost to the ground. For more information on these and other cross-country ski trails, pick up a Hayward Area Ski Trail Guide at local businesses.

For snowmobilers, Sawyer County has a whopping 600 miles of trails; adjacent Washburn County has an additional 144 miles. For maps, contact Sawyer County, (800) 472-3474 (WI) or (800) 826-3474 (U.S.), and Washburn County, (715) 635-2886.

Exploring the backcountry on snowshoes.

BAYFIELD

Perched on the shore of the world's largest inland lake, Bayfield's setting is as much of a draw as its array of winter activities. Take it all in by visiting Mt. Ashwabay, a downhill and cross-country ski area with great views of sprawling, frozen Lake Superior. The hill has 11 runs and a chalet; rentals and lessons are available. Cross-country skiers can ride up the slope on the T-bar and start their trek high, or take off from the chalet and circumnavigate the hill. Mt. Ashwabay is on Ski Hill Road, off Highway 13 south of Bayfield (715-779-3227). West of Washburn on County C, the Teuton and Valkyrie trails tempt cross-country skiers with a quieter experience and rugged terrain reminiscent of the Western mountains (715-373-2667).

When conditions permit, the ice caves at Squaw Bay are worth searching out. Here, sheets of frozen water create spectacular formations in the intricate sandstone caves. To get to them, however, you must walk, snowshoe or ski along the edge of frozen Lake Superior. Be sure the lake is frozen! Best conditions are usually in February; check with the Apostle Islands National Lakeshore office (715-779-3397) before setting out. Dog-sledding and winter camping trips around the Apostle Islands are offered by Trek & Trail outfitters (800-354-TREK). And Bayfield itself is a lovely outpost to explore. Many of the shops are open year-round, and driving the "ice road," which rides atop the lake from the town dock to Madeline Island, is always a thrill.

Off the peninsula but worth noting is the cluster of ski areas near Hurley. Whitecap Mountain, with 33 runs, is one of Wisconsin's largest downhill complexes (800-933-SNOW). Unusually varied, it offers descents from three different hills, along with views of scenic rock outcroppings. Four more downhill slopes—Indianhead Mountain, Big Powderhorn, Blackjack Ski Resort and Porcupine Mountain State Park—lie across the state line in Michigan.

An unusual historic trail awaits cross-country skiers at the town of Montreal. A small system of loops wraps around the site of an old iron mine; interpretive signs detail its history. Nearby, the Uller Trail, perhaps the state's most remote cross-country ski trail, takes off from Highway E. This beautiful 16-mile, linear route, which transects the wild Penokee Range, starts on the side of a road and ends on the side of a road, with no road in between. The Uller is not groomed and, because it lies in the Lake Superior snow belt, is frequently obliterated, leaving you to follow blue blaze marks on the trees. Be sure to check the weather report before you set off, and carry emergency supplies. Call (715) 561-4334 for information on both the Montreal and Uller trails.

Bayfield County has 600 miles of snowmobile trails; Iron and Ashland counties provide an additional 500 miles. For trail maps and conditions, call Bayfield County, (800) 472-6338; Ashland County, (715) 264-3000; and Iron County (715) 561-2922.■

An early snowmobile.

HISTORY OF THE SNOWMOBILE

The world's first snowmobile was built in the heart of Wisconsin's North Woods, in the little town of Sayner in Vilas County. To carry himself over the snowdrifts, Carl Eliason set a toboggan on front and rear tracks, then powered the craft with a small gasoline motor. He patented the machine in 1927. The following year, Joseph Bombardier of Quebec invented a snow machine with two outer tracks and a central enclosed car.

The machines proved very useful, especially to trappers, wardens, power company repairmen and others who needed to get about to do their work, but they were not especially sporty. It wasn't until the 1950s and '60s that the flashy cruisers hit the woods. With a growling roar, snowmobiling quickly became a fad. Today it's a full-fledged, highly popular sport.

To learn more about the history of snowmobiling, and to view antique and contemporary machines, visit the Vilas County Historical Museum in Sayner. It's free, and open daily spring through fall.

CITIES
for all
seasons

World-class museums, gracious

parks, lively neighborhoods,

 interesting shops—

Milwaukee lures visitors

with modern attractions

in an Old World setting.

Madison, our state capital,

charms us with its natural

beauty, refined cultural tastes

and a relaxed attitude that

welcomes all.

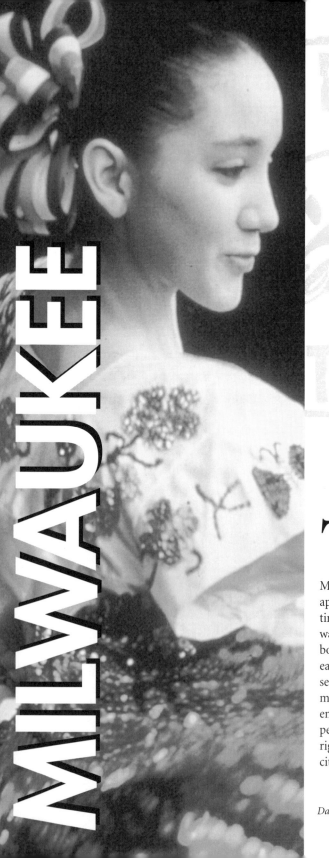

MILWAUKEE

Milwaukee, Vibrant and Diverse

The late Pulitzer Prize-winning novelist Edna Ferber wasn't born in Milwaukee, yet she was able to appreciate the city in the short time she lived here with a warmth usually found in the born and bred. Writing in the early 20th century, Ferber seemed struck by the city's melting-pot quality: "You encountered all the kinds of people there are in the world, right there in the middle-sized city of Milwaukee, Wisconsin."

Her words have lost none of

Dancer at Mexican Fiesta.

their aptness. There is a sense of variety in the natives of the largest city in Wisconsin—not cosmopolitanism, nothing that smacks of false sophistication. The inhabitants are savvy and at the same time unassuming, embracing the Old World values system and mores on which the city was built.

When Milwaukee was incorporated in 1846, contingents of Germans, Poles, Italians and Irish were setting down roots in homogeneous pockets in the North, South and West sides. All that's left of those mini-communities is an ethnic grocery here and a family-owned shoe repair shop there. But amid an ever-changing landscape, they are visual reminders of the city's beginnings and evidence that progress doesn't have to completely shroud the past. When visitors come to Milwaukee, they find a city that has never lost sight of its infancy, a city that is thoroughly modern, yet undeniably historic.

OUTDOORS

In the 19th century, the waterworks and sewerage system, of all things, shaped a significant part of Milwaukee's landscape: The first public parks were created with sanitation as much as Sunday strolling in mind. A more concerted effort to build a parks system took place later in the century. In 1889, a group of zealous politicians appointed a commission to develop a chain of parks, and create, in the poetic words of one leader, the "lungs of the city." Among the parks the commission pushed for is Lake Park, planned by Frederick Law Olmsted's cele-

Milwaukee easily mixes the old and the new.

brated firm, which also designed New York's Central Park. Today, well-maintained Lake Park is an East Side beauty mark, and the only park whose grounds are graced by a gourmet French restaurant, Lake Park Bistro.

The Milwaukee County Parks System now has more than 150 parks and parkways on nearly 15,000 acres of land, offering everything from indoor and outdoor ice skating, in-line skate hockey, cross-country skiing, sledding and ice fishing in winter, to indoor and outdoor swimming, tennis, golfing and (yes) croquet and lawn bowling in summer. A small sampler of

Henry Maier Festival Park.

the pleasures awaiting: Humboldt Park (3000 S. Howell Ave.) and its rare lotus garden, with plants imported from India; Whitnall Park (5879 S. 92nd St.), a haven for night skiing and boffo toboggan runs; Dretzka Park (12020 W. Bradley Rd.), the site of one of only a handful of 18-hole disc golf (a glorified name for Frisbee)

courses in the state. Call the Parks Information Line, (414) 257-6100, for details.

Whitnall, the county's largest park at 660 acres, is home to two manmade treasures. Wehr Nature Center (9701 W. College Ave., Franklin; 414-425-8550), an environmental education facility with programs for children and adults, offers great hiking opportunities that won't scare off weekend walkers. Boerner Botanical Gardens (5879 S. 92nd St.; 414-425-1130) features an outdoor formal garden, open spring through fall, and an indoor garden house that's a must for plant buffs— the yearly agenda is always stacked with events like Victorian tree workshops and wreath-making classes.

Also of note is Trimborn Farm Park, Milwaukee County's only historic park (8881 W. Grange Ave., Greendale; 414-529-7744). Werner Trimborn produced lime from baked limestone on this 1850 farm estate, which is listed on the National Register of Historic Places. During the holidays, it's transformed into a 19th-century winter wonderland. Think of Victorian decorations, craft items and trees for sale, and you've got the right idea. The property includes the restored 1847 Jeremiah Curtin House, open only in summer.

Exceptional public golf

courses are at Brown Deer (7835 N. Green Bay Rd.), which hosts the celebrity-loaded Greater Milwaukee; Whitnall (5879 S. 92nd St.); Oakwood (3600 W. Oakwood Rd.); and Dretzka parks (12020 W. Bradley Rd.). Call (414) 643-5100 for information.

Mitchell Park Horticultural Conservatory (a.k.a. "The Three Domes") is an irresistible draw for out-of-towners and a fun place for local families, who make pilgrimages to the annual special shows. Three massive glass-domed greenhouses (524 S. Layton Blvd.; 414-649-9800) display arid, tropical and seasonal plants. The seasonal dome has five theme shows a year, while the arid and tropical domes brim with thousands of plant species from around the world. An institution since 1964, the conservatory is open 365 days a year.

It isn't often that you're dumped smack-dab in the middle of suburbia and yet feel utterly detached from the clatter of everyday life. But Schlitz Audubon Center at 1111 E. Brown Deer Rd. in Bayside (414-352-2880) has this oasis-like essence that somehow distances it from the deer-filled residential area almost completely surrounding it. The 225-acre nature sanctuary has hiking trails, ponds and prairies, plus hands-on projects for kids, nature exhibits

St. Josephat's Basilica.

and the serene border of the Lake Michigan shoreline.

The beaches have a magnetic attraction. Lake Michigan stretches like a glorious blue blanket, a summons during the warm months, a gulf of rocky trouble in the winter. In summer, residents flock to Bradford Beach (2400 N. Lincoln Memorial Dr.), Doctors Park (1870 E. Fox Lane) and South Shore Park (2900 S. Shore Dr.) to cool off, the young, bronze and bikini-clad dominating the ranks. And in early spring,

Milwaukee River.

anglers who practice the art of smelt fishing (purists say "schmelt") can be spotted in the wee hours of the morning in lakeshore coves.

ARCHITECTURE

The architecture in Milwaukee's residential and commercial neighborhoods is eclectic, with many Queen Annes, Victorians and English Tudors. The backgrounds of the city's early architects was equally broad. German-born Henry C. Koch, for example, left a European (Romanesque/ Queen Anne) stamp on the

many churches and courthouses he designed. In contrast, Massachusetts-born George Bowman Ferry, who designed the Pabst Mansion, took his cues from English and Flemish Renaissance architecture. Built for brewery president Frederick Pabst, the opulent mansion at 2000 W. Wisconsin Ave. has 37 rooms, 14 fireplaces and priceless ornamental ironwork, and is considered Milwaukee's outstanding residential landmark. For tour information, call (414) 931-0808.

In the first half of this century, the designs of Wisconsin

EATING WELL

Karl Ratzsch's—If there's an enduring misconception about Milwaukee, it's that eating out means strictly German food. But it is true that the city has at least three fine German restaurants. Of these, the deservedly most famous is Karl Ratzsch's, featuring liver dumpling soup, buttery veal schnitzel and tender sauerbraten. 320 E. Mason St. (414) 276-2720.

Sanford—Restaurateur Sandy D'Amato has consistently been heralded for his work by magazines such as Bon Appétit and organizations like the American Institute of Wine & Food. His gourmet, European-style storefront restaurant, Sanford, has created the definitive description of dining—quality, attention to detail and presentation.1547 N. Jackson St. (414) 276-9608.

Grenadier's—German-born chef Knut Apitz's landmark of French and continental cuisine is close to impeccable. 747 N. Broadway. (414) 276-0747.

The King & I—Some of the hottest curries this side of the Orient. 823 N. Second St. (414) 276-4181.

Au Bon Appétit—The pita bread, hummus and lamb rarely get better in America than at Au Bon Appetit. 1016 E. Brady St. (414) 278-1233)

Bartolotta—Serious pasta lovers who don't mind plunking down a chunk of change will adore the splendid Bartolotta. 7616 W. State St. (414) 771-7910.

Three Brothers—Eastern Europe is a burek away at this Old World-flavored restaurant, housed in a turn-of-the-century tavern. 2414 S. St. Clair St. (414) 481-7530.

Arteaga's—The enchiladas are almost as extraordinary as the kitschy Elvis paraphernalia. 1234 S. 16th St. (414) 671-5360.

LODGING

Pfister Hotel—Going to the hilt means going to the Pfister, which proves that beauty remains with age. Built in 1893, the elegant hotel has 307 rooms and enough distractions—nightclub, espresso bar, pool, fitness center—to keep the weary traveler indoors. (414) 273-8222.

Wyndham Milwaukee Center—Renovated in 1993, the Wyndham is about as state-of-the-art as hotels go, a space holding 221 rooms and 77 suites. Another reason to set down the luggage here: The Wyndham is adjacent to the Theater District complex and across the street from the Marcus Center for the Performing Arts. (414) 276-8686.

Milwaukee Hilton—Formerly known as the Marc Plaza, the 500-room Hilton sits in the core of downtown, within walking distance of Grand Avenue shopping mall, restaurants and taverns. (414) 271-7250.

Marie's—This bed and breakfast inn in Bay View, a few miles south of downtown, has four antique-laden rooms, a shared bath and morning meals weighted with sweets baked by owner Marie Mahan. (414) 483-1512.

Washington House Inn—Listed on the National Register of Historic Places, Washington House Inn, in charming Cedarburg about 20 minutes north of Milwaukee, has 34 rooms, all but three of which have whirlpools. A continental breakfast is prepared from turn-of-the-century recipes. (414) 375-3550.

EVENTS

Summer Festivals—Milwaukee is the "City of Festivals," and summer is its busy season. For details on Summerfest, Polish Fest, Asian Moon Fest, Irish Fest and other ethnic celebrations, see the chapter "Great Summer Festivals."

Grape Lakes Food & Wine Festival—Wine auction, gourmet dinner, seminars, 5K run and walk hosted by the Milwaukee Art Museum. Held in May.

Audubon Art Fair—More than 100 artists display their works at the Schlitz Audubon Center; entertainment and nature programs, too. Held in June.

Miller Lite's Ride for the Arts—One of the largest bicycle rides in the country with routes of 5 to 50 miles. Held in June.

Lakefront Festival of the Arts—Close to 200 artists set up at Lakefront Park. Held in June.

Milwaukee Journal/Sentinel Rose Festival—Display of 50,000 roses, workshops and entertainment at Boerner Botanical Gardens. Held in June.

Great Circus Parade—Authentic re-creation of a circus street parade with restored circus wagons. Held downtown in June.

Holiday Folk Fair International—International cuisine, culture exhibits and workshops, with 60 ethnic groups represented. Held in November.

Winterfest—Olympic-size outdoor skating rink, family activities, figure-skating exhibitions and ice-sculpting at Cathedral Square. Held in December and January.

For more information, call the Greater Milwaukee Convention and Visitors Bureau, (414) 273-7222 or (800) 231-0903.

A sampling of the fare at neighborhood taverns.

WATERING HOLES WITH MOXIE

Imagine a bowling lane with balls the size of a fist and diminutive pins positioned at the end of 16-foot lanes. That's Koz's Mini-Bowl (2078 S. Seventh St.; 414-383-0560), a Formica-topped bar-cum-bowling-alley where even a klutz can roll spares. Known affectionately as the train-car bar, Midwest Hiawatha (366 E. Stewart St.; 414-481-5480) is a tavern perfectly maintained in a stationary railroad lounge car complete with cheesy music and cheesier service. Everybody's drinking cocktails at At Random (2501 S. Delaware Ave.; 414-481-8030), where the menu teeters in the 100 range and the drink of lovers is the two-strawed Tiki Love Bowl flambé. For people who like a little intrigue, the Safe House (779 N. Front St.; 414-271-2007) is open only to those who know the password; inside, the spirit of mystery hangs over every nook and cranny.

native Frank Lloyd Wright were emulated by some of his state-based protégés, though credit for the work sometimes mistakenly later went to Wright. The East and West sides of Milwaukee were the territory of Russell Barr Williamson, an Indiana-born Wright apprentice who, in the early 1920s, created some of the cleanest Prairie-style lines in the city. His work and that of others is easily viewed by taking a walking or driving tour. Historic Milwaukee (414-277-7795), a local organization dedicated to preserving the historic face of the city, offers outdoor guided tours when the weather cooperates. For brochures and information, call the Greater Milwaukee Convention and Visitors Bureau (414-273-7222) or the Milwaukee County Historical Society (414-273-8288), itself housed in a 1913 landmark bank building at 910 N. Third St.

SPORTS

Milwaukeeans are a rational lot; they save emotional outbursts for the appropriate times, e.g., sporting events. And fans from this part of the state are far from the fair-weather type. Locals were behind the Milwaukee Brewers when they won the American League baseball pennant in 1982 and have stayed supportive through the inevitable losing streaks. For ticket information, call (800) 933-7890. The same goes for Milwaukee Bucks basketball, tickets for which are a hot commodity at the Bradley Center, the site of their home games (1001 N. Fourth St.; 414-227-0500). It isn't just the sight of a fight that gets fans' blood boiling for Milwaukee Admirals hockey; it's the camaraderie in the stands. The Admirals also play at the Bradley Center. Indoor soccer is on the level of spectacle. The Milwaukee Wave team packs kids and quite a few adults into the Bradley Center by playing rock music at high-decibel level, along with some pretty aggressive "football," as Europeans call it. Call (414) 962-9283 for ticket information.

THEATER

Aficionados of local theater had reason to rejoice when the Baroque opera house-inspired Broadway Theatre Center was finished in 1993 (158 N. Broadway; 414-291-7811). It meant that several homeless theater groups had finally found some permanent digs and that, with a little luck, legions of the drama hungry would frequent the historic Third Ward area just south of downtown Milwaukee, the scene of a small-caliber artistic and commercial renaissance. The center's tenants are Skylight Opera Theatre, whose curious repertoire mixes opera

Pabst Theater.

and Broadway musicals (414-291-7800); the cutting edge Theatre X, a small Obie-winning group that often presents company-developed plays (414-278-0555); and Milwaukee Chamber Theatre, which produces North America's only theater festival devoted to playwright George Bernard Shaw (414-276-8842).

The largest professional theater company in the city is Milwaukee Repertory Theater,

Milwaukee County Historical Center.

of *A Christmas Carol* (144 E. Wells St.; 286-3663).

Other audiences can find their niche at various venues. For the Puccini crowd, it's the Florentine Opera, which brings in national and international performers for shows at the Marcus Center for the Performing Arts and the Pabst Theater (414-291-5700). For the Barney set, Great American Children's Theatre, a national touring company, features productions like *The Lion, the Witch and the Wardrobe* (414-276-4230). First Stage Milwaukee Theatre for Children presents shows that range from classic to contemporary, with productions aimed at specific grade levels (414-273-7206).

MUSEUMS

When it comes to art, Milwaukeeans are anything but uncouth. The city has two nationally known institutions: Milwaukee Public Museum, a showplace of natural history artifacts, and Milwaukee Art Museum, featuring more than 20,000 works from the 15th century to the present. Since 1882, Milwaukee Public (800 W. Wells St.; 414-278-2702) has specialized in walk-through exhibits. Highlights include the "Streets of Old Milwaukee" (look for the old woman in the perpetually moving rocking chair), the award-winning "Costa Rican

which offers classic, modern, cabaret and holiday productions in a three-stage complex called the Theater District (108 E. Wells St.; 414-224-9490). On the Wells Street side of the complex is the historic Pabst Theater, whose musical and theatrical acts range from Guy Lombardo's Royal Canadians to the Milwaukee Rep's staging

Rainforest" and "Exploration Station," a hands-on science exhibit. Milwaukee Art Museum (750 N. Lincoln Memorial Dr.; 414-224-3200) also has a few pieces that may stick in viewers' heads forever: Wisconsin artist Georgia O'Keeffe's "Poppies," Jules Bastien-Lapage's 1881 painting "Père Jacques (The Wood Gatherer)," and Duane Hanson's disturbingly realistic 1973 life-size sculpture of a janitor.

Not all the art bases are covered at the Big Two Museums, however. Smaller, less-trafficked museums are jewels for particular interests. Take the Brooks Stevens Automotive Museum (10325 N. Port Washington Rd. 13W, Mequon; 414-241-4185), for example. Vintage autos (rare Packards, Cadillacs and Excaliburs) are on view from the collection of the late Milwaukee industrial designer Brooks Stevens, a man perhaps best known for designing the Oscar Mayer Weinermobile. Children have two choices for their amusement and education—and both should satisfy their parents' demands for quality entertainment. Discovery World Museum in the Milwaukee Public Library (818 W. Wisconsin Ave.; 414-765-0777) is chock-full of interactive exhibits and weekend workshops. The Betty Brinn Children's Museum (929 E. Wisconsin Ave.; 414-291-0888) bills itself as the place

A taste of Milwaukee's international feast.

ETHNIC GROCERIES

Around South 16th Street and West National Avenue on Milwaukee's South Side, a Chicano beat takes over. Inside Mercado El Rey (1023 S. 16th St.; 414-643-1640), nary a word of English is spoken but the language of food, of course, is universal. Produce and spices like jicama, cilantro and chili peppers are everywhere, plus fresh meats, a bakery serving the buttery pastry known as churro, and a small carryout cafe. At A&J Polish Deli (1215 W. Lincoln Ave.; 414-643-7733), half the floor is occupied by a linear butcher case stocked with fresh sausage and cheese; the other half is a mini-supermarket lined with canned goods and Warsaw periodicals. Gingerroot and ginseng are a tag team at The Asian Mart (1125 N. Third St.; 414-765-9211), which carries hard-to-find ingredients for everything from egg rolls to egg foo yung.

"where learning means hands-on fun." Kids can, for example, watch golf balls loop, spin and race over ramps—and thus learn about momentum, friction, acceleration, speed and distance. Targeted at children ages 1 to 10, the museum also hosts workshops for parents; music, dance and storytelling programs for kids; and traveling exhibits.

Documenting the struggles, history and culture of African Americans, America's Black Holocaust Museum displays photos of lynchings in the South, and other hauntingly brutal artifacts, with unapologetic frankness (2233 N. Fourth St.; 414-264-2500). The founder is Milwaukee author James Cameron, an African American who himself survived a lynching. Opened in 1988 and patterned after the Jewish Holocaust Museum in Jerusalem, the museum uses books, photographs and commentary as illustrative tools.

Never a shortage of good loaves.

FRESH-BAKED BREAD

Bread is a phenomenon in Milwaukee, and with several stores in competition there's never any shortage of good loaves. Three stores are tops for crusty, European-style breads: La Campagne (10050 N. Port Washington Rd. 13W; 414-241-6305), with an unusual flax/sesame seed bread and flaky rosemary rolls; Breadsmith (2632 N. Downer Ave.; 414-962-1122), featured in *Bon Appetit* for an outstanding French peasant loaf; and Daily's (4001 N. Oakland Ave., 414-962-6100; 8775 N. Port Washington Rd., 414-351-6511; 16005 W. Blue Mound Rd., 414-785-1101), which turns out magnificent sourdough breads and rolls, plus solid sandwiches, soups and desserts. For softer whole-grain bread and giant cookies, the shop worth stopping for is Great Harvest Bread Co. (5629 N. Lake Dr., 414-963-9690; 13404 Watertown Plank Rd., Elm Grove, 414-821-0118).

SHOPPING

Milwaukeeans seem to balance their appreciation for the convenience of mall shopping with the old-fashioned simplicity of contiguous stores in plein air. Packs of such shops are located in different sectors of the city.

What for a long time was undeveloped land in Brookfield is now a mass of upscale women's clothing stores, salons, bookstores, gourmet grocery stores and restaurants. At the head of the heap is the splurgy food emporium V. Richard's at 17165 W. Blue Mound Rd. (414-784-8303), Milwaukee's 360-degree turn from budget grocery shopping. For clothing that appears just off the runway but sells for off-the-rack prices, visit Loehmann's at 17135 W. Blue Mound Rd. (414-785-2606).

In a northern suburb of Whitefish Bay, you'll find Au Courant (400 W. Silver Spring Dr.; 414-963-1950), which stocks Giorgio Armani for women; Zita (205 E. Silver Spring Dr.; 414-332-0126), where Joan Collins could have upgraded her "Dynasty" wardrobe; Schwanke-Kasten jewelers (324 E. Silver Spring Dr.; 414-964-1242), Milwaukee's Tiffany's without the attitude; and Just Kidding (318 E. Silver Spring Dr.; 414-962-2524), just the spot to turn a 2-year-old into a pint-size fashion plate.

In Mequon, the buzzword is upscale along the intersection of North Port Washington and West Mequon roads. Specialty shops in strip mall-like developments range from Allen-Edmonds (11043 N. Port Washington Rd. 13W; 414-241-4266), the maker of nationally sought-after men's and women's leather footwear, and Erik of Norway (1505 W. Mequon Rd. 112N; 414-241-

5111), where massages and facials are the first order of business, to Pam Kozlow Petites (1515 W. Mequon Rd. 112N; 414-241-8944), which caters to women under 5 feet 4 who'd rather die than dress like a little girl.

There's an element of history on North Jefferson Street, between East Mason and East Wells streets. The block is anchored by the venerable George Watts and Son (761 N. Jefferson St.; 414-291-5120), in business since 1870. In addition to the china patterns, crystal and sterling silver for which it is known, Watts has the city's only tea room, a superb upstairs chamber serving a tasty chicken salad and to-die-for homemade English muffins. Next door, Scandinavia (767 N. Jefferson St.; 414-276-7226) imports fine contemporary furniture from the Nordic countries, including a delightful platoon of Swedish Santas for collectors. The commercial tone changes down the street—from flower shop to coffeehouse to eclectic tavern—boasting just that variety that Edna Ferber was talking about. ■

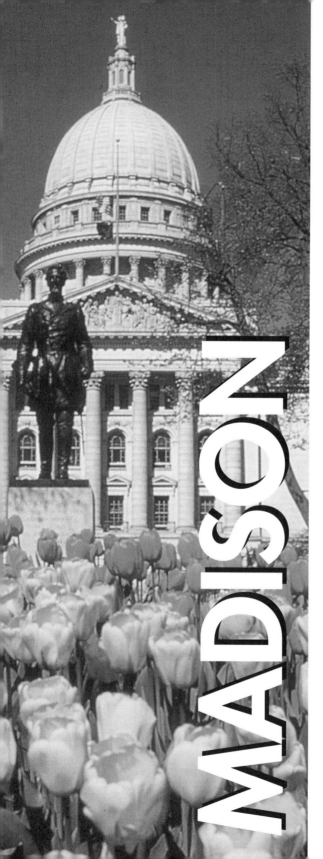

MADISON

In a Madison State of Mind

The tale of a newcomer captivated by Madison is so common, it has almost become a truism. What is the city's charm?

For many, it is the natural beauty: four handsome lakes and more than a hundred parks. For others, it's all the opportunities to hear concerts, attend plays, dance, listen to lectures, and watch athletic events—most of them (by big-city standards) inexpensive, many of them free and all, in a town of less than 200,000, near at hand.

And underneath Madison's refined cultural tastes, lies another beguiling aspect: its small-town roots. Here, around the city's most sophisticated emblem, the Capitol building, area farmers market their vegetables, cheese, fresh poultry and home-baked bread. On Saturday nights, square dancers kick up

The Capitol gardens in bloom.

their heels to the fiddle and the banjo in an open-air pavilion near the heart of the city. And at the University of Wisconsin-Madison, the largest public university in the country, workers churn out 75 flavors of home-made ice cream.

STREETSIDE

The life of a city is in its streets, and in Madison the liveliest byway is State Street. In the 1970s, the city banned all traffic, except buses, from this thoroughfare, turning it into a successful urban mall.

State Street is a paradise for those who love intimate restaurants and small, locally owned shops. Here you'll find Himalayan, Greek, Italian and Continental cuisine, as well as entire stores devoted to soaps, used books, vintage clothing, pets, bicycles, posters, outdoor gear, coffee and trendy street-wear. But State Street is also a wonderful historical setting.

Look up, beyond the modernized ground floors, and on building after building you'll see the graceful details of 19th- and early 20th-century architecture—reminders of the capital city's long history as a center of commerce. At 302 State St. (now the Triangle Market), you'll find a delicate brick turret, built in 1899. At State and Mifflin are two of the several flatiron buildings constructed in the 1850s to accommodate the angled

crisscrossings of the isthmus streets. And at 125 State St. (now the Glaeve Gallery) is one of the most exquisite examples of terra cotta ornamentation left in Madison. On this circa-1850 building (one of the city's first firehouses built plainly and ornamented in 1922), engravings of white

State Street.

Grecian urns, cornucopias, lilies and the stern face of a bearded old man wind gracefully around the shop's window frames and doors.

And, of course, at the very peak of State Street is the gorgeous Capitol building itself, built between 1906 and 1917, and featuring 43 varieties of decorative stone, finely carved wood furniture and the most spectacular view in the city. Unlike other towns, which sprung up at a port or river crossing, Madison is a created city, selected in 1836 to be the political center of the Wisconsin Territory and platted—supposedly in 48 hours—by early developers. Climb the spiral stairway to the

Olbrich Botanical Gardens.

walkway around the Capitol dome, and notice the city's orderly layout between lakes while birds fly by at eye level.

Today the Capitol grounds, with beautiful gardens and stately trees, forms the splen-

did setting for Madison's most popular community events: the Art Fair on the Square, a July event that draws 500 exhibitors from throughout the Midwest; Concerts on the Square, the Wisconsin Chamber Orchestra's series of free Wednesday evening outdoor concerts; and the Saturday morning Farmers' Market.

At the other end of State Street, you'll find nourishment of a different sort—the University of Wisconsin-Madison, a premier educational institution whose libraries and other learning resources are open to any state resident. Stop by the Geology Museum in Weeks Hall (1215 W. Dayton St.; 608-262-2399), which houses an extensive collection of meteorites, precious stones and fossils, including a 10,000-year-old mastodon skeleton found by farm boys in a creek bed near Boaz, a community in southwest Wisconsin. View the fine collection of Asian, ancient Greek and contemporary art at the Elvehjem Museum (800 University Ave.; 608-263-2246). Refresh body and mind at the Allen Centennial Garden (intersection of Observatory and Babcock drives), where you'll find dazzling display gardens composed of hundreds of labeled plant species. On Saturday mornings at Vilas Hall, laugh till the tears roll at "Whad'Ya Know," a nationally syndicated radio program hosted by the irrepressible Michael Feldman; for ticket information, call (608) 263-4141 or (800) 942-5669. And for a real treat, visit the Washburn Observatory (608-262-9274) on Bascom Hill on the first or third Wednesday of the month. When skies are clear, the observatory opens its doors to the public, as it has for the last hundred years, and volunteers train the old telescope on the most interesting objects in the night sky.

Of course, there is more to Madison than downtown. Mansion Hill just off the Square, with its elegant 19th-century homes, makes a great place to stroll on a hot summer day. Nature trails are just moments away at the UW-Madison Arboretum (608-263-7888), a thousand-acre retreat of wetlands, hardwood forest and tallgrass prairie on the southwest side. Olbrich Botanical Gardens at 3330 Atwood Ave. (608-246-4551) contains more than 50 acres of beautiful demonstration gardens and a glass dome overrun with tropical plants. A fun way to tour the city is to hunt down the works of a former Wisconsin resident—architect Frank Lloyd Wright. Few American cities have as many realized Wright buildings as Madison. His local work includes seven homes and the First Unitarian Meeting House at 900

University Bay Drive, a soul-stirring church building. Look for Wright and Wright-influenced homes in the University Heights neighborhood, wedged between University Avenue and Regent Street on the near west side.

LAKESIDE

After newspaper editor Horace Greeley visited Madison in 1854, he described this lakeside city as having "the most magnificent site of any inland town I ever saw." To capitalize on the publicity, Madison developers, who were agggressively seeking new settlers, promptly gave the city's lakes mellifluent Indian names ("Mendota" was said to mean "great" and "Monona," "beautiful.") The lakes have been Madison's drawing card ever since.

Lake Mendota is a sailor's delight, and on warm summer days hundreds of brightly colored boats ply the sprawling waters. Both Mendota and Monona are popular spots for power boating; the lakes are big, they have stunning views of the Capitol, and you can motor from one to the other through the locks at Tenney Park.

For a quieter, more intimate experience, slide your craft into Lake Wingra. Power boats are not allowed on this small, spring-fed lake, so you can sail or paddle without fear of overpowering wakes, or simply

Gathering at Memorial Union Terrace.

SIT AND SIP WHILE THE CITY WALKS BY

While you're in Madison, be sure to indulge in the classic city pastime—people watching. Victor Allen's Coffee & Tea, 401 State St., has the best streetside location, with big picture windows on two sides of a triangular building. Up on the Square, grab a coffee or an egg roll from one of the street vendors, snare a bench along the sidewalk, and watch the world (or at least the state legislators) walk by.

If a glass of wine and a view of boaters pulling in sounds right, try the outdoor bar and grill at the Edgewater Hotel, 666 Wisconsin Ave., along Lake Mendota. And for the most Madisonian experience, wander over to the terrace of the UW Memorial Union, the favorite hangout of students, alumni and just about everybody when the sun is out and the air is balmy. On your way there, sample some of the dairy school's own ice cream, sold in the Union's front lobby.

drift near the wooded shoreline and poke through the marshes. Rent your canoe at Wingra Canoe and Sailing Center, 824 Knickerbocker (608-233-5332). Lake Wingra is also a popular site for sailboarding; an outfitter at Vilas Park Beach rents boards and gives lessons.

Because of its setting, Madison hosts a number of sailing regattas, crew races and other lake-related events. For unforgettable entertainment, check out the looney Paddle and Portage (held in July), in which two-person teams paddle a one-mile course on Lake Mendota, portage their canoe 1.3 miles across the isthmus at the Capitol Square, then paddle another two miles on Lake Monona.

Landlubbers can enjoy the lakes in plenty of other ways. Pedal around Lake Monona on an 11-mile designated bikeway that winds along quiet residential streets. Or go for a stroll on the shaded Lakeshore Path that stretches two and a half miles from the UW-Madison Memorial Union to Picnic Point, itself a spot worth exploring. This wooded peninsula jutting into Lake Mendota contains quiet walkways, some of the best birding in the area and even an old apple orchard left over from the days when the university grew its own fruit. The low, spreading branches of the trees make perfect places for

Madison's magnificent setting.

EATING WELL

L'Etoile—This fine dining establishment prepares creative cuisine that features the best ingredients the Midwest has to offer. 25 N. Pinckney St. (608) 251-0500.

The Blue Marlin—Another premier restaurant with elegant fresh fish and seafood dishes. 101 N. Hamilton St. (608) 255-2255.

Kennedy Manor Restaurant and Bar—Tucked into a landmark apartment building near the Square, Kennedy Manor specializes in upscale comfort food like roast chicken and house-made ravioli. 1 Langdon St. (608) 256-5556.

Quivey's Grove—Housed in an 1855 stone house and stable, Quivey's captures the essence of Wisconsin in regional-heritage dishes named after the state's historic personalities. 6261 Nesbitt Rd. (608) 273-4900.

Smoky's Club—Slabs of perfect steaks; homemade soups, hash browns and pickled beets, too. 3005 University Ave. (608) 233-2120.

Pasqual's—Stop here for top-notch burritos, posole and blue-corn tortillas. 2534 Monroe St., (608) 238-4419 and 2098 Atwood Ave., (608) 244-3142.

Ella's Deli and Ice Cream Parlor—

Kids especially enjoy the musical toy collection—and the kosher hot dogs and sundaes. 2902 E. Washington Ave. (608) 241-5291.

Dotty Dumpling's Dowry—Juicy burgers and terrific mouth-filling sandwiches. 16 N. Fairchild St. (608) 255-3175.

LODGING

Mansion Hill Inn—Eleven sumptuous rooms, valet service, whirlpools and fireplaces in a sandstone Italianate mansion. (608) 255-3999)

The Livingston Inn—A stunning Gothic Revival home, built in 1857, with four rooms. (608) 257-1200.

Arbor House—An "environmental inn" (once a stagecoach stop) near the UW Arboretum. (608) 238-2981.

Hotels and motels—A number offer suites, pools and in-house restaurants: Best Western Inn on the Park (608-257-8811; 800-528-1234), the Concourse Hotel (608-257-6000) and the Edgewater (608-256-9071) are on or near the Capitol Square.

EVENTS

Dane County Farmers' Market—Saturdays, May through October, from 6 a.m. to 2 p.m. at the Capitol.

Cows on the Concourse—

Kick-off for June Dairy Month around the state, with live bovines and dairy treats.

Concerts on the Square—Bring a picnic and relax on the Capitol lawn while the Wisconsin Chamber Orchestra performs. Held in Wednesdays in June and July.

Rhythm and Booms—The Midwest's largest fireworks display lights up Warner Park on the Fourth of July.

Art Fair on the Square—Nearly 500 artists from throughout the Midwest. Held in mid-July.

Maxwell Street Days—Bargains from State Street vendors; food and entertainment too. Held in mid-July.

Paddle and Portage—A zany canoeing contest on two lakes, with a portage across the isthmus. Held in July.

International Holiday Festival—Celebration of Dane County's cultural diversity, with music and dance at the Madison Civic Center.

Holiday Flower Show—Hundreds of poinsettias and a miniature village with model trains, at Olbrich Botanical Gardens.

For more information, contact the Greater Madison Convention & Visitors Bureau, (800) 373-6376.

Saturday morning Farmers' Market.

breezes, and listen to the restful lap of water against shore.

NIGHTSIDE

If it's a more vibrant sound you're after, then explore the city at night, when it comes alive with music, song, laughter and dance.

You can watch the world's best performers at the Wisconsin Union Theater (608-262-2204), hailed as one of the country's finest venues when it opened in 1939. Its lakeside setting, art deco interior and superb acoustics still captivate.

World-class artists also perform at the Madison Civic Center (608-266-9055), a renovated vaudeville and movie palace on State Street. The interior was gutted in the 1970s and replaced with a multi-level structure that knits a rich and eccentric past with contemporary sensibilities. You can watch touring ballet companies and Broadway productions from the plush seats of the chandelier-lit Oscar Mayer Theater, or enjoy the city's own professional Equity group, the Madison Repertory Theatre, in the sleek Isthmus Playhouse.

As for local artists, once a year the Madison Savoyards stage a Gilbert and Sullivan play that is consistently polished and uproarious. The Wisconsin Chamber Orchestra (608-257-0638) and the Madison Symphony Orchestra (608-257-3734) both play

reading, sunbathing and, of course, picnicking.

When you're walking along the isthmus, be sure to keep an eye out for the city's "street-end" parks. In these diminutive greenspaces (at the end of Livingston Street on Lake Mendota, and off Few and Ingersoll streets on Lake Monona, for example), you can rest on a bench under a shade tree, catch the lake concert series. And if you like small ensembles, don't miss a performance by the Pro Arte Quartet. This group was the string quartet to Her Majesty Queen Elizabeth of Belgium when it first came to Madison more than 50 years ago to play in the Wisconsin Union Theater. After Germany invaded Belgium, the UW brought the quartet to campus permanently. Though its members have changed over the years, the ensemble is considered one of the five best string quartets in the world.

ESPECIALLY FOR KIDS

With its lakes and parks, Madison seems designed for kids. But even so, there are a few other special attractions. The Madison Children's Museum, 100 State St. (608-256-0158), is a hands-on discovery station for the little ones. The Henry Vilas Zoo, in Vilas Park (608-266-4732), houses lions, elephants, bears, monkeys and, in the children's area, adorable baby animals, along with a multitude of other creatures. For astronomy info straight from the experts, bring the kids to The Space Place, 1605 S. Park St. (608-262-4779). Featuring displays and lectures, it's operated by the UW's Astronomy and Space Science department, one of the world's most renowned space research centers. ∎

Relaxing on campus.

BEST BETS FOR BARGAIN ENTERTAINMENT

For the best entertainment bargains, head for the university campus. You can groove to live jazz, rock and international sounds for free in Union South's Red Oak Grill and in the Memorial Union's Rathskeller on Friday and Saturday nights. For classical music, check out what's happening at Mills Concert Hall, where the Wisconsin Brass Quintet, the Symphony Orchestra and other groups perform. (Tickets are generally under $5 and sometimes free.) The Union Directorate runs a travel movie series throughout the year at the Wisconsin Union Theater.

Because the university itself is so broad-ranging, on any given weekend you're likely to find a number of other diverse and unusual events—an Indonesian gamelan concert, for example, lectures on health, philosophy, politics or literature, or an African dance festival. Consult *Wisconsin Week*, the university's newspaper, or *Isthmus*, Madison's free alternative weekly, for details.

great summer FESTIVALS

Ah, summer. Time to wake up and smell the sweet corn— and the Limburger, the lefse and the tamales. There are enough festivals in Wisconsin to keep you eating, as well as dancing, singing, listening and learning, all season long. Can't control that craving for chocolate? Grab a dessert (maybe three or four) at Burlington's Chocolate City Festival. Is your back yard bereft of roses? Sniff the 50,000 blooms at the Milwaukee Journal/Sentinal Rose Festival at Boerner Botanical Gardens. Maybe you'd like to commune with aliens? You might find a few—or at least a few wannabes—at Elmwood's UFO Days. Celebrate strawberries, hamburgers, bratwurst, logging, art, catfish, even twins. Honor Wisconsin's wonderfully diverse heritage, too, at scores of ethnic gatherings. To get you started, here are 35 of the state's best festivals.

AEBLESKIVER FEST, LUCK

If you eat an *aebleskiver* in May you're bound to be in Luck—the town of Luck, that is, in Polk County. This Danish delicacy—described as "round as a tennis ball, richer than a waffle, bettter than a pancake"—has been drawing hungry people to the West Denmark Lutheran Church here, during the first week of May, for more than 30 years. Smothered in butter, syrup and grape jelly, *aebleskivers* are served in the evening with ham, sweet soup and *aeblekage* (apple cake). Local residents also sell Scandinavian crafts and baked goods. (715) 472-2195.

FESTIVAL OF BLOSSOMS, DOOR COUNTY

Home to a million daffodils ("Doorfodils") and uncountable numbers of wildflowers, Door County bursts into bloom during the month of May. To celebrate, the county holds a month-long Festival of Blossoms that includes a lighthouse tour, art show, shipyard tours, Door County's largest parade, ethnic celebrations, Blossom Ball and

A few of Door County's "Doorfodils."

senior golf tournament. The county's state parks offer naturalist-led and self-guided wildflower walks. And a map published by the Chamber of Commerce leads you to some of the area's outstanding private and public gardens. (414) 743-4456.

FOLK FESTIVAL, ASHLAND

This event, sponsored by Northland College, is the longest-running folk festival in the state. It kicks off Friday evening with an open stage on which anyone can get up and play, followed by a professional act and square dance. Saturday's activities include workshops, a craft fair and an evening headline concert. The festival occurs the second weekend of May. Be sure to buy tickets in advance since seating is limited. (715) 682-1289.

WHITE BLOSSOMS/ BLACK POWDER FESTIVAL, GAYS MILLS

Surrounded by more than a thousand acres of apple trees in full bloom, Gays Mills offers a near-perfect setting for a spring celebration. To view—and smell—the blossoms, take a walk or a wagon ride through the Kickapoo Orchard on the edge of town. Later, watch the life-size pup-

pets at the Thread of Life puppet show. Round out the weekend with a visit to the flea market, the folk music stage and the black powder rendezvous, where pioneer re-enacters demonstrate American life in the 1800s. The festival takes place on Mother's Day weekend. (608) 735-4341.

CHOCOLATE CITY FESTIVAL, BURLINGTON

If you possess a weakness for chocolate, this festival could have serious consequences for your waistline. Vendors here sell chocolate desserts in all their delectable variations, from chocolate-covered strawberries to chocolate eclairs. Nestle Foods, the city's largest employer, also unveils a "chocolate creation"—a look-but-don't-eat sculpture made from 2,000 pounds of pure chocolate. A carnival, crafts fair, music and the Chocolate Parade add garnish. The festival takes place the weekend after Mother's Day. (414) 763-6044.

SYTTENDE MAI FOLK FESTIVAL, STOUGHTON

On May 17, 1814, Norwegian leaders signed their country's first constitution. Though independence from Sweden didn't come until many years later, that date still carries significance to Norwegian communities everywhere, including Stoughton in Dane County, which commemorates it annually at its Syttende Mai ("Seventeenth of May") celebration. The largest event of its kind outside of Norway, this is also one of the oldest, tracing its roots to 1868. Whether your last name is Olsen or O'Leary, you'll find plenty to see and do here, from sampling *blo-kulb* (blood baloney) and other hearty Norwegian dishes to watching the world-famous Stoughton High School Norwegian Dancers. You can test your endurance in the three-mile Norse Canoe Race or the 20-mile Syttende Mai Run. Afterwards, visit the rosemaling exhibit, where artists demonstrate the traditional painting technique. (608) 873-7912.

Morel mushroom.

MOREL MUSHROOM FESTIVAL, MUSCODA

From a botanical standpoint, the morel is just another fungus. From a culinary standpoint, however, it's a delicacy worthy of celebration. And since the morel proliferates in the countryside surrounding Muscoda, it makes perfect sense that this community of 1,300 throw a party in its honor on the third weekend of May. The hard-core set out on foot to hunt down the elusive fungus, but you don't have to crawl around in the woods to enjoy the event. Stop by downtown Muscoda to sample morels, rolled in flour and fried in butter, and be on hand to witness the popular Mushroom Contest, which awards prizes to the largest, oddest and heaviest specimens. Festivities also include a crafts fair and carnival rides. (608) 739-3154.

JUNE

GREAT WISCONSIN CHEESE FESTIVAL, LITTLE CHUTE

The story begins in 1988, when the town of Rome, New York, held a competition that ranked the Empire State's cheddar ahead of the Dairy State's. The following year the people of Little Chute invited the mayor of Rome to a rematch. Wisconsin's cheddar won hands down at that com-

Syttende Mai parade.

petition; Little Chute has been celebrating the victory ever since. Among the highlights of the Great Wisconsin Cheese Festival: a cheese-carving contest, Big Cheese Parade, volleyball tournament, cheesecake contest, craft booths and children's rides. The event is also an opportunity to sample every variety of cheese made in Wisconsin. It's held the first weekend in June. (414) 788-7390.

CANAL DAYS, PORTAGE

Named after the waterway that once provided a key transportation link between the Great Lakes and the Gulf of Mexico, Canal Days features a carnival, arts and crafts fair, juried art show, collector car show, kids' fisheree, flea market and a full music schedule. Saturday's parade is the highlight of the weekend. A tractor pull and canoe races round out the entertainment. The festival is held the first weekend in June. (800) 474-2525.

BAYFEST, GREEN BAY

This four-day affair, the second weekend in June, runs on a simple formula: good music + good food = good times. With five stages showcasing some of the nation's finest jazz, blues, folk, funk and fusion musicians, and 25 international and domestic food tents offering everything from Jamaican jerk chicken to Mo Shu Pork, Bayfest has little trouble living up to its claim as "the biggest celebration of food and music north of Milwaukee." Also on tap is a carnival, fireworks, arts and crafts show, hole-in-one golf tournament and a variety of kids' activities. (414) 465-2145.

STRAWBERRY FESTIVAL, WAUPACA

Strawberry shortcake is the focus here, though there is nothing short about this cake—nearly 500 feet of sponge cake, whipped cream and freshly picked berries. No appetite? No problem. Activities for the not-so-hungry include a 10K run, a strawberry recipe contest, a model railroad display, a children's costume contest and live music. The festival takes place the third weekend in June. (800) 236-2222.

WALLEYE WEEKEND FESTIVAL, FOND DU LAC

Though the Mercury Marine National Walleye Tournament is the focal point of this event, which takes place on the second weekend in June, there are so many other things going on that you might not even notice. Foremost among them is the World's Largest Fish Fry. In the sport's category, there's the state's largest volleyball tournament, a three-on-three hoops tournament, the Walleye Run/Walk and milk-carton boat races. Feeling lucky? Grab a club and take a swing at the $100,000 Hole-in-One Shoot-Out. Four stages feature music for all tastes, and a main stage headlines national entertainment. Familyland offers a slew of children's activities to keep the young ones entertained. (414) 923-6555.

CESKY DEN, HILLSBORO

Since 1983, Hillsboro's Cesky Den or "Czech Day," has offered some of the best Czech cuisine and music this side of the Bohemian Forest. A midday banquet, which begins at 11:30 a.m. on the second Saturday of June, features roast pork, sauerkraut, *knedliky* (potato) dumplings and *rohleke* (rye rolls). Afterwards, diners hit the dance floor for a calorie-burning polka session or sit back and listen to the sounds of the Yuba Hillsboro Czech Singers. A polka Mass rounds out the heritage celebration. (608) 489-3192.

FYR-BAL FESTIVAL, EPHRAIM

Each Father's Day weekend, Ephraim's shore is ablaze with bonfires as the town celebrates the summer solstice with ancient Norwegian traditions. The bonfires burn the winter witches (figuratively, of course) and welcome the secretly selected Fyr-Bal Chieftain, who arrives by boat from the dark waters of Lake Michigan. In addition to Saturday night's ceremony, the Fyr-Bal (as in "fire ball" but pronounced "fear ball") offers a host of other activities, including a fish boil, book sale, folk-dancing demonstrations and live entertainment. (414) 854-4134.

MILWAUKEE JOURNAL/SENTINAL ROSE FESTIVAL, HALES CORNERS

More than 350 varieties of roses will be on display during this celebration at Boerner Botanical Gardens. For nine days, starting the third week in June, experts will hold workshops on flower photography, horticulture, wreath-making and flower arranging. Also scheduled are outdoor concerts, ethnic dancing and children's entertainment. Be sure to stroll through the 40-acre garden, home to an elegant assortment of perennials, wildflowers and herbs, and the country's largest collection of crabapple trees. (414) 529-1870.

GREAT WISCONSIN RIVER LOGJAM, WAUSAU

Even if history class put you to sleep, this "week-the weekend following Father's Day weekend. (715) 848-6143.

MUSKY FESTIVAL, HAYWARD

Hayward has been musky-mad since 1949, when two fishermen in a three-month period landed world-record muskies, each weighing nearly 70 pounds. In celebration of that remarkable summer, the community reaches deep into its tackle box of attractions to lure visitors to its Musky Fest, held the third weekend in June. Fish are a central part of the festivities, with fishing contests and seminars. Activities also include a

pageant, arts and crafts show, three-on-three basketball tournament, 10K run, carnival and sidewalk sale. (715) 634-8662.

GREEK FESTIVAL, RACINE

The Lake Michigan shoreline bears little resemblance to the rugged coast of Greece, but at Racine's Greek Festival all it takes is imagination to find yourself in a festive taverna. The Greek Orthodox Church hosts a feast on the last full weekend in June that includes everything from *spanakopita* (a spinach and feta cheese pastry) to roast lamb to *loukomathes* (hot honey puffs). Music, folk dancing, cooking demonstrations, rides and games round out the celebration. (414) 632-5682.

Berlin Victorian Days.

VICTORIAN DAYS, BERLIN

This event showcases Berlin's 25 Victorian homes, which can be seen on two different walking tours held the last weekend in June. After the tours, stop by Nathan Strong Civil War Park, where costumed re-enactors put on a mock Civil War battle and artisans sell their wares. Other attractions include bluegrass and folk music, Civil War exhibits and a book sale. (414) 361-3636.

JULY

BELGIAN DAYS, BRUSSELS

This celebration of Belgian culture, held on the first weekend after the Fourth of July, places a heavy emphasis on food: People come from far afield—even Belgium itself—to eat *jutte* (cabbage fried with nutmeg), *trippe* (pork and cabbage sausage) and other Belgian dishes. The feast is served on Sunday, a day that also includes a 10K run, parade, music, and arts and crafts. Saturday is reserved for "Belgian baseball," slow-pitch softball in which the bases are run in the reverse direction. (414) 825-7007.

BAY DAYS, ASHLAND

Nationally syndicated deejay Mike Harvey kicks off the festival activities on the third weekend in July with a live broadcast of his popular Super Gold Show. From there, it's three days of music, food and activities. The music schedule features popular regional acts; the athletic schedule includes a 60K bike race, 10K run, three-on-three basketball tournament and a sailboat race. A crafts fair and kids activities run throughout the festival. (800) 284-9484.

ART FAIR ON THE SQUARE, MADISON

In booths set up on Madison's beautiful Capitol Concourse, nearly 500 artists from around the country display artwork in diverse media, including ceramics, glass, photography, wood and leather. The art fair, held the second weekend in July and sponsored by the Madison Art Center, is juried so quality is assured. Four stages and dozens of food booths provide diversion. (608) 257-0158.

TWIN-O-RAMA, CASSVILLE

In what may be the most creative excuse to throw a party, Cassville's Twin-O-Rama, held the third weekend in July, features more than 500 twins, some of whom travel from as far away as Europe to attend. The event, which began in 1929 as a twins picnic, offers a double dose of fun, with carnival rides, a parade, fireworks and plenty of good food and music. Sunday is the highlight of the weekend, as twins compete for trophies in such categories as Look-Most-Alike and Look-Least-Alike. (608) 725-5037.

HOLLAND FESTIVAL, CEDAR GROVE

Take off those Air Jordans, put on a pair of wooden shoes, and join in the fun at Cedar Grove's annual Holland Festival, on the last Friday and Saturday of July. Each day the streets are scrubbed, and Klompen Dancers march in full costume down Main Street. On Friday, wooden-shoe races are followed by musical performances and the serving of the World's Largest Worstebroodje (pig-in-a-blanket). Saturday's activities include a parade and the Holland Festival Run/Walk. There is also an arts and crafts fair, ethnic foods and a performance by the Holland Fest Players. If you've misplaced

your wooden shoes, you can purchase a pair at the festival. Be sure to bring along a few pairs of socks for cushioning. (414) 457-9491.

UFO DAYS, ELMWOOD

Whether you're seeking a close encounter with an unidentified flying object or merely a good time, be sure to visit Elmwood. The self-proclaimed UFO Capital of the World, this farming community has developed an international reputation as a magnet for extraterrestrials (one observer theorized, "They feel safer in the country"), and has attracted the likes of Oprah Winfrey, Geraldo and Dan Rather. Sightings seem to have thinned out in the last decade, however. The three-day celebration, held the last full weekend of July, includes a fun run, pancake breakfast, cow-chip throwing contest, street dance, kids activities and, on Sunday, a parade, for which locals don aluminum antennae and smear themselves with green face paint. If you go, be sure to try the UFO burger, a cheeseburger smothered in sauerkraut. (800) 474-3723.

AUGUST

HERITAGE FESTIVAL, IRON COUNTY

This 17-day celebration, held the first two weeks in August, showcases Iron

County's natural and historic attractions, as well as its Finnish, Italian, Cornish and Native American heritage. Bicyclists, hikers and paddlers can sign up for the festival's Flambeau Trail Trek, a five-day journey from Madeline Island to the Turtle Flambeau Flowage along a historic route used by Native Americans and fur traders. Runners can participate in the Paavo Nurmi Marathon, named after a famous Finn who won nine Olympic gold medals. Other events include historical walking tours, concerts, ethnic meals, parades and art shows. (715) 561-2922.

On the Flambeau Trail Trek.

BRATWURST DAYS, SHEBOYGAN

This isn't *a* bratwurst festival; it's *the* bratwurst festival. Sheboygan, the self-acknowledged Bratwurst Capital of the World, serves up three tons of the succulent sausage on the first full weekend in August. The hungry and/or competitive belly up for the bratwurst-eating contest, and, to facilitate digestion, beer flows freely (there is an alcohol-free site as well). Four stages offer continuous entertainment. (414) 457-9497.

HOME OF THE HAMBURGER CELEBRATION, SEYMOUR

Hamburgers are commonplace at most summer festivals, but the patty grilled at Seymour's annual August celebration is rare by any definition. Organizers here turn out a burger of prodigious proportions; the whopper in 1989 tipped the scales at 5,520 pounds, a world record. Why all the hamburger hype? In 1885, Charles Nagreen, a.k.a. "Hamburger Charlie," a New London resident who happened to be in Seymour, squashed a meatball between two pieces of bread. Thus, the hamburger was born and the world was changed forever. Festivalgoers at this one-day event, held the first week in August, celebrate Charlie's genius by consuming the big burger or participating in a 10K Bun Run and the Hamburger Games, which include such events as a ketchup slide and bun toss. (414) 833-7511.

FIREMEN'S CATFISH FESTIVAL, POTOSI

They may be charged with putting out fires, but the firemen in Potosi can cook a pretty mean catfish as well. Batter-fried and served with chunky potato salad and cole slaw, the catfish is so delicious more than 2,000 pounds are consumed over the course of the day. Other festivities include: Little Miss Catfish Queen contest, arts and crafts show, volleyball tournament, canoe races, fireworks and car- nival rides. The festival is usu- ally held the second week of August. (608) 763-2481.

OTTO GRUNSKI POLSKI FESTYN, MENASHA

Otto Grunski was: (a) a courageous leader of the Polish resistance in World War II. (b) a famous Pole who died in 1975 after devouring 52 kielbasa in 15 minutes. (c) the legendary but unacknowl- edged inventor of the Bone Shaker, an aptly named precur- sor of the modern bicycle.

The correct answer is "c," at least according to the people of Menasha, who have been throwing a festival in Otto's honor since 1972. Though you won't come across Otto's name in the history books, you will find plenty of Polish good times if you stop by Jefferson Park for this affair, held during the second week- end of August. Otto's Wacky Wheels Parade and the two- mile or 10K Grunski Runski top a busy schedule that includes an experimental bike show, softball tournament, and polka and folk dancing. (414) 725-4822.

GREAT RIVER TRADITIONAL MUSIC AND CRAFTS FESTIVAL, LA CROSSE

Dust off your mandolin, tune up your banjo, and head to La Crosse for the annual Great River Traditional Music and Crafts Festival. During the day, the festival offers workshops and mini- concerts on everything from folk dancing to flatpicking. At night, musicians perform old favorites and new tunes. Regional artisans sell their work and demonstrate their skills. Children's activities abound, and food booths serve samples for every palate. The festival is held the week- end before Labor Day. (608) 782-3033.

SWEET CORN FESTIVAL, SUN PRAIRIE

For four days during the third week of August, Sweet Corn Festival organizers steam more than 60 tons of the vaunted vegetable, attracting 100,000 hungry visitors. Though corn is the big draw, visitors find time between feedings to see the Cornfest Parade on Saturday morning and the midget-car races later that night. A carnival, with crafts fair and live music, runs throughout the festival. (608) 837-4547.

SEPTEMBER

WISCONSIN STATE COW CHIP THROW, PRAIRIE DU SAC

Lighter than a discus and more natural than a Frisbee, cow chips can be flung great distances. It takes a strong arm, however, to win the State Cow Chip Throw—the current record is a hurl of 248 feet. The prestigious competition, which occurs on the Saturday of Labor Day weekend, is open to all. If you enter, be sure to choose your meadow muffins carefully; experts say the best ones are dry, lightweight and about 6 inches in diameter. Besides the main event, weekend activities include a Tournament of Chips Parade, bovine bingo (where you bet on the placement of a wandering cow's fresh pie), a "cow pie" eating contest, an arts and crafts fair, a kids' tractor pull and 5K and 10K runs. (608) 643-4317.

WILHELM TELL FESTIVAL, NEW GLARUS

In New Glarus, seeing a performance of "Wilhelm Tell" on Labor Day weekend is a bit like watching "It's a Wonderful Life" on Christmas: Most viewers know how the story turns out, yet they still find meaning in its message. For more than 50 years, the people of this Swiss community have celebrated their proud heritage by acting out Friedrich Schiller's famous play. The drama, which tells the story of the Swiss struggle for independence in the 13th centruy, includes the notable scene where Wilhelm Tell is ordered to shoot an apple from his son's head after failing to show due respect to the governor's hat. The play is presented in English on Saturday and Monday, and in German on Sunday. Other weekend events include an art fair and Alpine Festival, with traditional Swiss music, dancing and yodeling. (608) 527-2095.

For a selection of festivals held in other seasons, see the chapters on Spring Flings, Autumn Rambles and Winter Escapes. For a more complete list of festivals, call the Wisconsin Division of Tourism, (800) 432-TRIP.

MILWAUKEE FESTIVALS

When it comes to celebrations, Milwaukee—the City of Festivals—is in a class by itself. From the Asian Moon Festival in June to the Native American Indian Summer in early September, Milwaukee can keep you singing, dancing and eating almost every weekend. All festivals are held at Henry Meier Festival Park on the lakefront, except Bastille Days, which is held on the streets of East Town.

Dressed up for Polish Fest.

JUNE

ASIAN MOON FESTIVAL
The largest multi-Asian festival in the country features classic and folk dance, arts and crafts, and demonstrations of cooking, martial arts, kite making, origami and calligraphy. Held on Father's Day weekend. (414) 273-5090.

POLISH FEST
Polka bands and folk dancers pick up the beat at Polish Fest. Pierogies—stuffed dumplings—provide sustenance. Held the third weekend in June. (414) 529-2140.

SUMMERFEST
A giant, 11-day party, Summerfest draws national acts and huge crowds. The festivities begin on the last Thursday in June. (414) 273-2680.

JULY

LA KERMESSE DE LA BASTILLE (BASTILLE DAYS)
Salute French culture at the continent's largest French festival, featuring a historic French village, long-bow competitions, can-can dancers in authentic costumes and four stages of continuous entertainment. The festival blends French and American culture with fashion shows and wine tastings. Held in mid-July. (414) 271-1416, (414) 223-7500.

FESTA ITALIANA
Pasta, pizza, cannoli ... need we say more? Held the third weekend in July. (414) 223-7877.

GERMAN FEST
An *oom-pah-pah* good time with traditional foods (try the *spanferkel*) and the best polka bands. Held the last full weekend in July. (414) 464-9444.

AUGUST

AFRICAN WORLD FESTIVAL
Celebrate the whole range of African-American culture, from traditional storytelling to hip-hop. Held the first weekend in August. (414) 347-0444.

IRISH FEST
Weep to the ballads, dance to the fiddles, partake of the tea. Held the third weekend in August. (414) 476-3378.

MEXICAN FIESTA
In commemoration of Mexico's Independence day, Mexican Fiesta celebrates Hispanic and Latin American music, art, food, crafts and dancing, and raises funds for college scholarships. Held the last week in August. (414) 383-7066.

SEPTEMBER

INDIAN SUMMER
Share Native American food, purchase handmade crafts, and join in powwow dancing at this colorful gathering. Held the second weekend in September. (414) 774-7119.

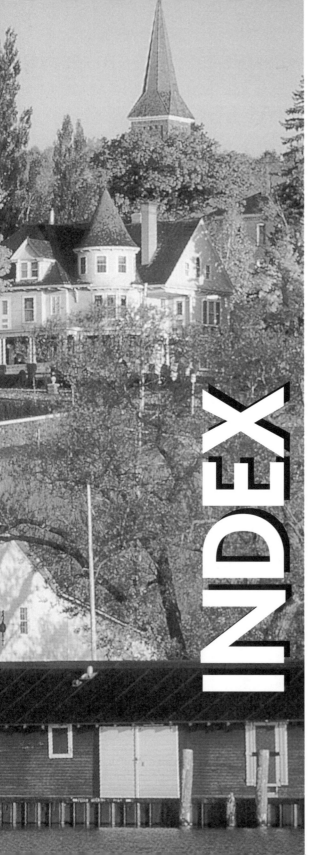

INDEX

INDEX

INDEX

INDEX

Whitnall Park, 130, 131
Wild Goose Parkway, 90
Wild Goose State Trail, 90
Wilhelm Tell Festival, 160
Williams Bay, 59
Willow River State Park, 95
Wilson House Inn, 77
Wine and Harvest Festival,
109
Winnebago Indian Museum,
22
Winterfest (Hayward), 121
Winterfest (New Glarus),
101
Winterfest (Milwaukee), 133
Winter Festival (Cedarburg),
109
Wisconsin Brass Quintet, 147
Wisconsin Chamber
Orchestra, 146
Wisconsin Dells, 19-23
Wisconsin Dells Polka Fest,
21
Wisconsin Maritime Mu-
seum of History, 41
Wisconsin River, 39
Wisconsin State Cowchip
Throw, 160
Wisconsin Union Theater,
146
Wolf River, 5
Wooden Boat and Maritime
Heritage Festival, 47
World Championship
Snowmobile Derby, 121,
122

Wo-Zha-Wa Days Festival,
21
Wright, Frank Lloyd, archi-
tecture of, 38-39, 134, 143
Wyndham Milwaukee
Center, 133

Y

Ye Olde Englishe Christ-
masse Feaste, 104
Yerkes Observatory, 59

PHOTO CREDITS: p. 2, George Archibald; p. 7, U.S. Army; p. 8, JRW; pp. 11, 13, 150, Door County Chamber of Commerce; pp. 21, 23, 62, Wisconsin Dells Visitor and Convention Bureau; p. 35, Bob Cyr; p. 38, Pedro Guerrero; p. 40, Glenn A. Oestreich; p. 41, William D. Hoard & Sons Co.; pp. 45, 47, B.W. Hoffmann; p. 65, Janet N. Heaton; p. 73, Bike Wisconsin; p. 74, A.R. McLaughlin; p. 87, Jim Harris; p. 90, Edgar G. Mueller; p. 105, Andy Coulson; p. 115, Russ Hoelscher; pp. 128, 132, Greater Milwaukee Convention and Visitors Bureau; pp. 129, 131, 136, Wisconsin Tourism Development; p. 130, Rutley; pp. 140, 141, 144, 145, 147, Jeff Miller, UW News Service; p. 149, Steve Sitter